A New Turn on Drunkard's Path

MARY SUE SUIT

Martingale™
& COMPANY

Dedication

To QUILTMAKERS AND quilt lovers everywhere: Our shared interest has led me down this intriguing path.

Acknowledgments

A SPECIAL THANKS to Judy Woodworth, Mary Lucas, and Becky Umenthum for the talents
and the time they have been willing to share.

CREDITS

PRESIDENT · *Nancy J. Martin*
CEO · *Daniel J. Martin*
PUBLISHER · *Jane Hamada*
EDITORIAL DIRECTOR · *Mary V. Green*
MANAGING EDITOR · *Tina Cook*
TECHNICAL EDITOR · *Karen Costello Soltys*
COPY EDITOR · *Allison A. Merrill*
DESIGN DIRECTOR · *Stan Green*
ILLUSTRATOR · *Laurel Strand*
COVER AND TEXT DESIGNER · *Trina Stahl*
PHOTOGRAPHER · *Brent Kane*

That Patchwork Place® is an imprint of Martingale & Company™.

A New Turn on Drunkard's Path
© 2002 by Mary Sue Suit

Martingale & Company
20205 144th Avenue NE
Woodinville, WA 98072-8478 USA
www.martingale-pub.com

Printed in Hong Kong
07 06 05 04 03 02   8 7 6 5 4 3 2 1

MISSION STATEMENT

We are dedicated to providing quality products and service by working together to inspire creativity and to enrich the lives we touch.

Library of Congress Cataloging-in-Publication data is available upon request.

ISBN: 1-56477-420-1

Contents

Introduction

BEING A LOVER of geometric quilt designs, I am fascinated by traditional Drunkard's Path quilts. However, I have a distinct aversion to using templates, so I've avoided exploring the possibilities of this intriguing design—until now. I found that by rotary cutting strips of fabric and then using a tool I developed, Mary Sue's Triangle Ruler™, to cut the strips into triangles and other shapes, I can create patchwork units that resemble traditional curve-pieced Drunkard's Path units (I call them drunkard's squares) without using a single template! All of the piecing becomes simple straight-line sewing. And, even better, this technique lets you double the number of fabrics used in each square, leading to many new design options and more interesting patchwork. More fabrics per square allows for a greater illusion of depth and motion in your quilt designs, giving a whole new meaning to a Drunkard's Path scrap quilt.

Lest you think this book contains remakes of traditional Drunkard's Path quilts, let me set you straight. What you'll find here is my technique for creating the look of a Drunkard's Path quilt without the work associated with templates and curved piecing (I seldom do windows either), along with my original quilt designs. While you can certainly apply my technique in a familiar Drunkard's Path setting, the projects in this book are meant to give you glimpses of the wider design potential of this interesting little patchwork square.

So, grab some fabric, your rotary cutter, and your rulers. Before you know it you'll be piecing a pathway of your own.

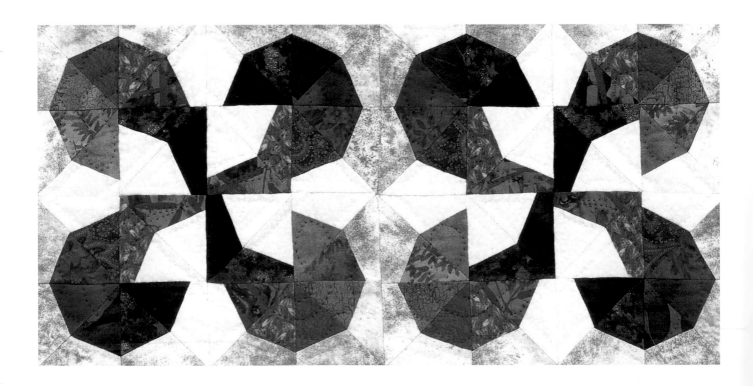

Using This Book

A QUICK GLANCE through this book will show you that the first thing you need to do is get acquainted with Mary Sue's Triangle Ruler and learn the cutting techniques. Everything you need to know about using the ruler is explained in "Cutting," starting on page 7. (Of course, if you don't have the ruler, you can make templates with the patterns provided on page 95. Your quilts will turn out just as lovely, but using the special ruler and a rotary cutter is definitely a time-saver.)

Piecing a drunkard's square is not difficult, and once you're adept at it (don't worry, it won't take long) you can choose a project and begin your journey. The drunkard's square can be made to finish at 2", 3", or 4", which means that each of the quilts can be made in three different sizes. The number of squares required and the number of individual pieces used in a project are the same for all three sizes. Only the initial strip sizes and finished quilt sizes are different.

Understanding the Shapes

EACH DRUNKARD'S SQUARE is made up of four pieces, rather than two pieces as in a traditional Drunkard's Path unit. While the square contains more pieces, it is quicker and easier to cut and assemble because no templates or curved seams are required.

The shapes used to construct a drunkard's square are two "kaleidoscope" triangles (I call them this because they are the same 45° isosceles triangles used to make a Kaleidoscope quilt block) and two mirror-image, four-sided "wings." The wings are cut from rectangles, and they look like skinny triangles with a tip cut off. (The shape is actually a quadrangle, but since quilters don't usually work with quadran-gles, it's easier just to call them wings!) I'll get into the specifics of cutting both of these shapes later. For now, it's good just to understand what they look like.

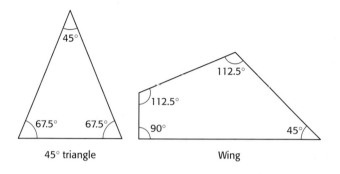

45° triangle   Wing

Using the Project Directions

THE INSTRUCTIONS FOR the individual quilts indicate the number of wing and triangle pairs to cut, but not the number of strips you'll need. That number varies depending on the size of the drunkard's square you choose. If you are making larger squares, you'll need more fabric strips. But whatever the size of the squares, the number of squares needed to make the quilt will be the same. Of course, all the measurements you'll need for each project are provided, including those for any setting squares or rectangles and for cutting mitered corners.

Before you decide which of the three sizes of drunkard's square to use in your project, I recommend that you make a test square in each size, to become familiar with the technique. Piecing all three sizes using the same fabrics will also let you see how the scale of the prints you're using will affect the look of the finished square.

Making Drunkard's Squares

A Simple Little Square Plus Variations

TRADITIONAL DRUNKARD'S PATH designs, as well as the quilt designs presented here, are based on just one little square. The traditional square is made up of a quarter-circle and a polygon with one concave side.

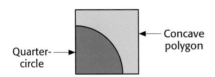

Quarter-circle

Concave polygon

Because my drunkard's square contains twice as many pieces as the curve-pieced block, you have the opportunity to shade the square with your fabric choices or to use just half a square. In the square shown below, two 45° triangles replace the quarter-circle, and the concave polygon is made up of two wings. Notice how the shading can dramatically change the look of the finished square.

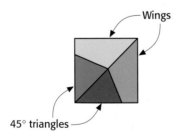

Wings

45° triangles

Half of a drunkard's square (one triangle and one wing) paired with a plain 90° triangle makes a different square, which can be used to expand the design possibilities. I refer to this unit as a half–drunkard's square.

Half–Drunkard's Square

Some of the quilt projects use additional squares or rectangles to round out the designs, but the drunkard's square and half–drunkard's square are the key elements in all the projects.

It's All in the Rotation

ALTHOUGH THE DRUNKARD'S square is simple in construction, quilt designs using it can be challenging to piece, simply because color-value placement is so important. The color-value placement within each square and the rotation of each square are critical to the success of the designs.

Most, but not all, of the designs in this book build from a four-patch unit made of four drunkard's squares. The units are repeated and rotated to make the larger blocks and connecting path squares.

Each four-patch unit can be rotated to create several different blocks. I make four identical four-patch units and then have fun seeing what develops by rotating each unit 90°.

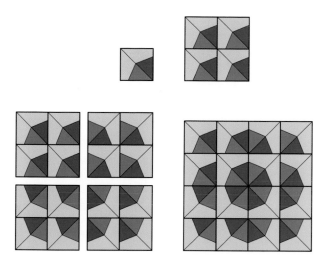

Rotating the four-patch units lets you develop totally different blocks. But it's also very easy to get the right square in the wrong rotation. (Trust me, I know!) If you want to make one of the projects so it looks just like the quilt shown, follow the color placement and four-patch rotation carefully. And remember that although it's easy to go astray, that can start you off on a wonderful new quilt design of your own.

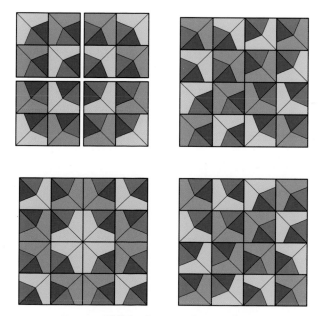

Four possibilities from one four-patch unit

Basic Square Construction

DRUNKARD'S SQUARES ARE made in a four-step process: cutting, sewing, pressing, and trimming. The directions below are for making a 4" finished square. However, the process is identical for the 2" and 3" squares; only the cut sizes of the fabrics change. On page 14 you'll find a handy conversion chart that shows you exactly what size to cut and how to measure for trimming your finished squares, whether they are 2", 3", or 4".

Cutting

DRUNKARD'S SQUARES CONSIST of mirror-image triangles and wings. The easiest way to cut them is to leave your rotary-cut fabric strips folded. That way, when you cut out the triangles and wings from the strips, you automatically have a left and a right for each shape. If you plan to use two different fabrics for the wings or for the triangles, unfold the two fabric strips; then layer them with same sides facing (either right sides together or wrong sides together, whichever you prefer). I layer mine with wrong sides together, so I am looking at the right side of the top fabric. The individual project instructions will tell you how many triangle pairs and wing pairs to cut.

Write Yourself a Note

IF YOU ARE using two different fabrics for the triangles or wings, write a note and leave it with your work to remind you which fabric goes on top and which sides are together when you cut the shapes. Doing this will help you place the fabrics in the same position every time you cut new strips, which is critical if you want the same fabric in the same position for each square.

WINGS

Two wings plus two 45° triangles make one drunkard's square. Except for the half–drunkard's square, you'll always need a pair of wings (a left wing and a right wing).

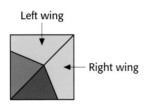

Left wing

Right wing

The wing pairs needed for the 4" x 4" square are cut from rectangles measuring 2½" x 8". How you cut the rectangles is up to you and the size and shape of your fabric pieces. Unless I am dealing with scraps and uneven pieces of fabric, I use one of the following two methods for cutting.

Method 1. With the fabric folded, cut a 2½" x 42" strip. Starting from the selvage edge, first trim off the selvages; then cut the folded strip into 8"-wide segments.

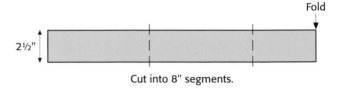

Fold

2½"

Cut into 8" segments.

Method 2. With the fabric folded, cut an 8" x 42" strip. Starting at the selvage edge, first trim off the selvages; then cut the folded strip into 2½"-wide segments. If your fabric is big enough to cut an 8"-wide strip, this method is the most fabric-efficient way to cut the rectangles.

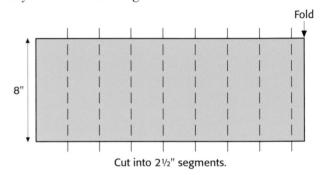

Fold

8"

Cut into 2½" segments.

For either method:

1. Lay a pair of rectangles (2 rectangles stacked same sides together) on your cutting mat with the 8" edges placed horizontally. If possible, place your cutting mat at the corner of a table so you can safely and easily cut from 2 sides of the table without having to rotate your fabric.

2. Place Mary Sue's Triangle Ruler on the rectangle with the 90° angle (the wide end) pointing to the right and the 2½" mark in the 90°-angle portion of the ruler aligned with the bottom edge of the rectangle. Align the 5" mark in the 45°-angle

portion of the ruler with the left edge of the rectangle.

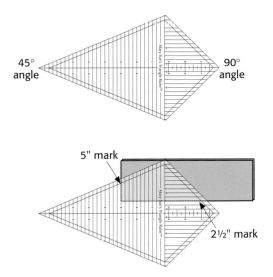

3. With the ruler accurately in place, cut along both its edges to make 1 pair of wings.

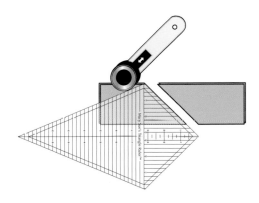

4. Remove the pair of wings you just cut, but leave the remaining fabric where it is. Rotate the ruler so that the 2½" mark is aligned with the top edge of the fabric and the 5" mark is aligned

with the right edge of the fabric. Cut along the ruler to create a second pair of wings.

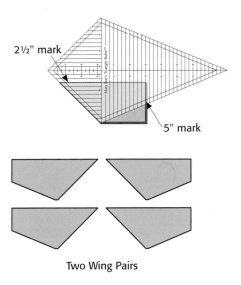

Two Wing Pairs

Cutting with a Template

If you are not using a Mary Sue's Triangle Ruler to cut your pieces, make a plastic template from the wing pattern on page 95. Lay the template on the rectangles as shown, and cut around it with your rotary cutter and ruler. Rotate the template and cut a second pair of wings from the rectangles. Note: A little bit of spray adhesive will help keep the template in place as you cut around it, but pay careful attention to the directions on the label for safe use.

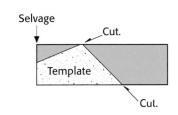

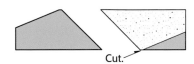

THE WING PIECES are cut in pairs as described above. When I am cutting a lot of wings at once, I stack three rectangles wrong side up and top them off with three rectangles right side up. This allows you to cut six pairs of wings out of the rectangles and easily separate them into wing and reverse wing piles three at a time, rather than individually.

Make sure your rotary cutter blade is sharp, and don't cut more layers than are comfortable for you. A dull blade or too many layers can skew the pieces, and hurt your wrist or shoulder.

45° TRIANGLES

While the 45° triangles don't look like mirror images, in order to have the outside edges of your finished squares be on the straight of grain, cut the triangles in pairs from layered fabrics, just as you did the wings.

1. With the fabric folded, cut a 3" x 42" strip. Using the folded fabric strip or 2 different fabric strips with same sides together, place the tip of the 45° angle of Mary Sue's Triangle Ruler at the top of the strips and align the center line of the ruler with the selvages. Make sure the center line is perpendicular to the cut edge of the strips. Cut along the ruler to establish the correct angle.

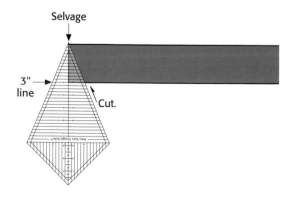

2. Align the crossbar with the previous cut, and place one of the ruler's 112.5° angles at the bottom edge of the fabric strips, as shown. Cut along the ruler to make 1 pair of triangles.

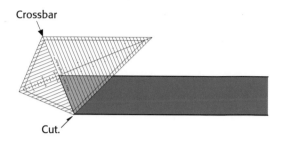

3. Align the crossbar with the previous cut and slide the ruler down so the ruler's other 112.5° angle is at the top of the fabric strips. Cut along the ruler to yield another pair of triangles. Continue cutting triangle pairs, rotating the ruler back and forth as you work your way across the strip.

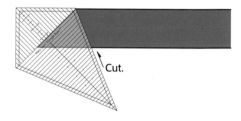

Cutting with a template:

If you prefer to use a template to cut the triangles, make a plastic template from the 45° triangle pattern on page 95. With fabric strips same sides together, place the template on the strips just inside the selvages, aligning one long side of the template with the upper edge of the strips. Cut along the template edges.

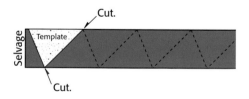

Without moving the fabric strips, rotate the template so that the long edge that was at the top for the last cut is now at the bottom. Cut along the template edge. Continue cutting triangle pairs, rotating the template back and forth as you work your way across the strip.

Piecing the Drunkard's Square

1. Lay out the pieces for the square on your sewing table, making sure the straight of grain in the triangles is along the outer edges of the square.

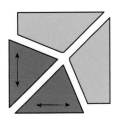

2. With right sides together, sew the right wing and the right triangle together. The tip of the triangle should extend slightly beyond the tip of the wing; the spot where the two pieces intersect should be ¼" from the sewing edge. Always sew from the wide end of the wing to the narrow end. (The wing may extend slightly beyond the triangle at the end of the seam. This extra fabric will be trimmed later.) Press the seam allowances toward the darker fabric.

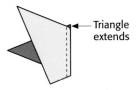

Triangle extends

3. Repeat the process for the left wing and left triangle; however, this time sew with the wing on the bottom. That way you are still able to sew from the wide end of the wing to the narrow end. Press the seam allowances toward the darker fabric.

Triangle extends

4. Match the wing seams; then sew the center seam to complete the square.

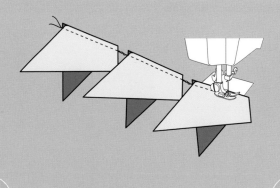

PRESSING IS ONE of the most important steps in piecing a quilt. Remember that the object of pressing is not to get the fabric warm but to make it lie flat. If you return to the sewing machine and notice that your pieced unit is not flat, press it again. Below are some tips that will help your drunkard's squares and quilt assembly go smoothly.

- Some quilters like to press the seam allowances open, but I prefer to press them to one side, to make hand quilting easier. I generally press toward the darker fabric.

- If pressing your seam allowances in either direction doesn't cause show-through, press the right halves of the drunkard's squares toward the wing and the left halves toward the 45° triangle. By pressing seam allowances in opposite directions, seams will lie flat when you sew the two halves of the squares together.

- If pressing the seam allowances to one side is creating too much bulk, try press-ing most of the length of the seam to one side, then pressing open just ⅜" or so at the end, where the unit will be joined to another.

- Before trimming the drunkard's squares, I stack the unpressed squares on the ironing board with the wings at the lower edge. Then I press the square open so the wing corner is at the lower left. I use this pattern consistently unless show-through occurs.

- The biggest thing to remember about pressing is that if you are consistent, the seams will butt against each other when you rotate the drunkard's squares to form four-patch units.

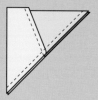

Press open with wings in lower left corner.

Trimming the Drunkard's Square

1. Place a drunkard's square on your cutting mat with the wing corner in the lower left, if you're right-handed. If you cut left-handed, you may find it easier to place the wing corner in the lower right.

2. Lay a Bias Square® or other square ruler on the square with 0 at the upper right corner. Align the ruler's diagonal line with the center seam, and place the ruler's 3½" marks at the wing seams. (Remember, these measurements are for the 4" drunkard's square only.) Trim any excess from the upper and right edges of the square.

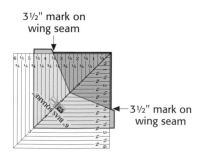

3½" mark on wing seam

3½" mark on wing seam

3. Rotate the square, placing the wing corner in the upper right. Then lay your ruler on the square with 0 at the upper right corner. Align the ruler's diagonal line with the center seam, and align the 4½" marks with the bottom and left edges of the square. Trim any excess from the upper and right edges to complete the square.

Piecing the Half–Drunkard's Square

SEVERAL OF THE quilt projects in this book use a half–drunkard's square as a design element. It's simply a square made up of one wing and one 45° triangle stitched to a plain 90° triangle. You can make it with either right or left wings and triangles so you can have mirror-image half–drunkard's squares.

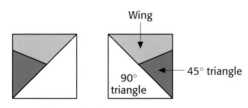

Half–Drunkard's Squares

1. Lay out the pieces for the square, making sure the 45° triangle has the straight of grain on the outside of the square.

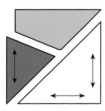 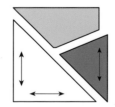

2. Sew the wing to the 45° triangle as for the regular drunkard's square. Press the seam allowances toward the darker fabric. Then sew the pieced unit to the 90° triangle. Press the seam allowances toward the darker fabric.

Trimming the Half–Drunkard's Square

1. Place a half–drunkard's square on your cutting mat with the wing pointing toward the lower left. Notice that this means a different orientation for squares made with right wings than for squares made with left wings.

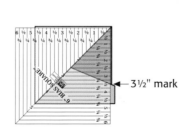

2. Lay a Bias Square or other square ruler on the square with 0 at the upper right corner. Align the ruler's diagonal line with the center seam, and place the 3½" mark of the ruler at the wing seam. Trim any excess from the upper and right edges of the square.

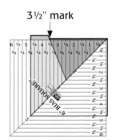

3. Rotate the square so that the wing points to the upper right.

4. Lay your ruler on the square with 0 at the upper right corner. Align the ruler's diagonal line with the center seam, and align the 4½" marks with the bottom and left edges of the square. Trim any excess from the upper and right edges to complete the square.

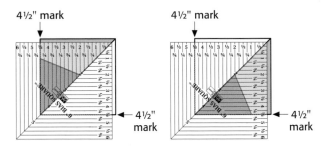

Cutting Guidelines for Squares of Various Sizes

THE CUTTING EXAMPLES in this chapter give measurements for a 4" finished square. Below, you'll find the measurements needed for squares in three sizes: 2", 3", and 4". The measurements indicate not only what sizes to cut your fabrics but also how to align your ruler for trimming of the squares.

Size of finished squares	2" x 2"	3" x 3"	4" x 4"
Size of unfinished squares (includes seam allowances)	2½" x 2½"	3½" x 3½"	4½" x 4½"
Size to cut strips for 45° triangles	2" x 42"	2½" x 42"	3" x 42"
Size to cut rectangles for wings	1½" x 5"	2" x 6½"	2½" x 8"
Ruler mark for cutting wings	6"	5½"	5"
Ruler mark for first trim of squares	2"	2¾"	3½"
Ruler mark for second trim of squares	2½"	3½"	4½"

Calculating Yardage

EACH PROJECT IN this book comes with a materials list that tells you how much fabric you need in order to make a quilt in the size you want. However, many of my students have asked for help calculating yardage requirements when they work on their own designs. I thought you might find it helpful, too.

Size of finished squares	45° triangles	Wings
2" x 2"	2" x 42" strip yields 12 triangle pairs	5" x 42" strip yields 13 rectangle pairs or 26 wing pairs
3" x 3"	2½" x 42" strip yields 10 triangle pairs	6½" x 42" strip yields 10 rectangle pairs or 20 wing pairs
4" x 4"	3" x 42" strip yields 8 triangle pairs	8" x 42" strip yields 8 rectangle pairs or 16 wing pairs

Mitered Corners

MOST OF MY quilts have miters somewhere. I like mitered borders, and I also frequently use what I call mitered corners, which are mitered sections within the pieced design. Here's how to make them.

1. Check the cutting dimensions chart in the project directions for 2 important numbers—the miter strip width and the miter mark. The strip width is generally the same as the unfinished block size. The miter mark tells how far to measure along the strip before making the cut.

2. If the miter mark is less than 8", you can usually use 1 strip of fabric and leave it folded to cut the miter. If longer pieces are needed, cut 2 strips and layer them with wrong sides together.

3. Remove the selvages, using a ruler to make sure your cut is perpendicular to the long edge of the strips.

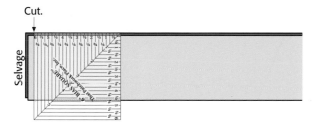

Cut Miter Strips First

IF YOU NEED to cut both miter strips and other pieces from a single fabric, cut the miter strips first; then cut any necessary rectangles or squares from the remainder.

4. Measure the correct distance from the cut edge of the fabric to the miter mark listed in the project directions. Make a mark on the bottom edge of the strips with a pencil or chalk.

5. Align the 45° diagonal line on your ruler with the upper edge of the strips so that the edge of the ruler runs directly through the miter mark on the fabric. Cut along the ruler edge.

6. Measure the correct miter mark from the diagonal cut at the top of the strip (the wide end of the angle) and make another mark. Cut perpendicular to the long edge of fabric at the mark.

7. Repeat to cut the desired number of miter pairs.

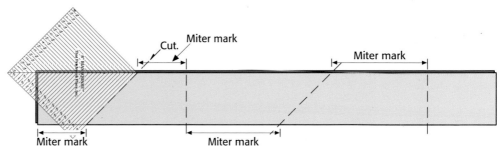

Techniques for Finishing

Let's face it. A quilt isn't a quilt until it's quilted and bound. In this section you'll find directions for adding perfect mitered borders as well as some guidelines for basting, quilting, and binding your project.

Adding Mitered Borders

Many of the projects in this book have a pieced border that helps finish or tie the whole design together. Others have a traditional outer border with mitered corners. Mitered borders are really quite simple, especially if you use my method for measuring and cutting to the correct length before attaching the borders to the quilt. Mitered borders are a sure-fire way to take your quilt's appearance from beginner to advanced in a few short steps, so I encourage you to try it.

1. Cut the borders to the lengths specified in the project directions. They allow a few extra inches in case your quilt size varies from the dimensions stated in the project directions. (You can always cut off extra fabric, but it doesn't look pretty when you have to add it on!)

2. Measure your quilt top from side to side, through the center, to determine the width. Write this number down.

3. Subtract ½" from the width measurement for seam allowances. The result is the finished width.

4. Divide your result from step 3 in half. For instance, if your quilt top measured 25¼" across, you would subtract ½" for seam allowances to get the finished width of 24¾". Dividing that in half (24¾" ÷ 2), the result is 12⅜".

5. Fold the border in half crosswise, with the fold at left.

6. Using the result you got in step 4 (half the finished width), measure from the fold along the bottom edge of the strip. Mark with a pencil.

7. Position a square ruler with its center diagonal line along the edge of the border and the ruler to the left of the mark so the ruler's right corner is aligned with the mark. Double-check your alignment; then cut along the ruler's edge. By cutting the folded border, you're cutting both of its ends at once, guaranteeing that both will be cut in the correct direction.

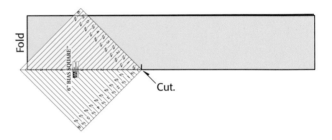

8. Cut another strip the same way for the bottom border. Then repeat steps 1–7 to cut 2 side borders; however, this time you'll be measuring the length of your quilt top.

9. Stitch the borders to the quilt in the order shown.

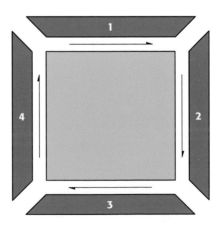

10. Starting at any corner, fold the quilt diagonally so the borders are right sides together and their edges are even. Sew the miter seam, starting from the inside and sewing to the outer edge. Press the seam allowances to one side (often, the fabric will let you know which way it wants to lie). Repeat for the remaining corners.

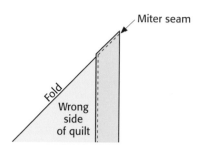

Miter seam

Fold

Wrong side of quilt

Preparing for Quilting

AFTER MUCH TRIAL and error, I have learned that before I even think about assembling the quilt layers, I need to press the quilt top one more time and check the back for errant threads that need to be trimmed. Make sure no dark thread tails or frays from fabric are long enough to show through a lighter section.

Marking

If you're planning to send your quilt to a professional long-arm machine quilter, most likely you don't need to mark the quilt top at all. That's something you should discuss with your quilter. If you'll be quilting on a frame or with a group, you probably want to mark the entire quilt top before it's layered and basted. If you'll be quilting in a hoop or on your own machine, you have the option to mark as you go.

I usually outline quilt ¼" from the seams. If several pieces join to form one design element, as with the flower petals in "Floral Bouquet" on page 60, I outline the entire design element rather than the individual pieces. I often quilt something within the elements too.

You can use ¼"-wide masking tape, available in quilt shops and catalogs, to mark straight lines. Rather than taping the entire top at once, position the tape as you quilt. You can usually reuse a piece of

tape several times before it will no longer stick well. Be aware that tape can be difficult to remove and may leave a residue if it is left in place too long.

I also like to use stencils. There are so many available that I always find something that works. I have used continuous-line machine-quilting stencils with great success. Borders make great places to use stencils. Graceful cables or other curved-line designs make a nice contrast to the straight-line piecing.

If your fabrics are light enough, you can use a very sharp, hard lead pencil to mark your design. Mark as lightly as possible. You can also use a water-soluble quilt-marking pen, but I've had difficulty removing the marks.

To mark dark fabrics, I prefer soap slivers. Save the little pieces of soap that haunt the bathroom and let them dry out. They work best when they are thin and hard. Avoid moisturizing soap bars as they may be oily. Soap helps the needle slide through the fabric and has usually disappeared by the time I have finished the quilting. If any soap remains, wipe it off with a damp cloth.

Basting

Whether you mark your quilt top before or after you baste the layers together, be sure that you do baste. The only exception is if your quilt will be quilted on a long-arm machine. Check with your quilter before spending time basting if it's not necessary. If you'll be hand or machine quilting at home, however, basting is essential.

1. Lay the backing fabric, wrong side up, on a flat surface. I use the living-room floor. Smooth out any wrinkles. I allow extra backing when hoop quilting, at least 2" on each side.

2. Spread the batting on top of the backing, making sure it lies flat. You may want to let the batting "breathe," or relax, before basting. If you're short on time, a quick toss in a tumble dryer set on low or air fluff can help remove any creases from packaged batting.

3. Lay the pressed quilt top, right side up, on top of the other 2 layers. Smooth out any wrinkles, making sure all 3 layers lie flat.

4. Using light thread and long basting stitches, baste from the center of the quilt to each corner. Fill in the remaining areas with basting rows spaced 4" to 6" apart. You can also baste using safety pins (use the same spacing between pins) or a quilt tacking gun.

5. If you quilt in a hoop or by machine, your quilt will be handled quite a bit. To protect the edges of the quilt top and batting, bring the excess backing around to the front and baste it in place to keep the quilt-top edges from fraying and the batting from stretching as you quilt.

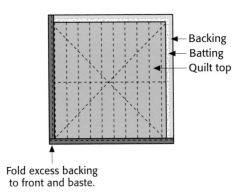

Fold excess backing
to front and baste.

Quilting

ONCE BASTED, THE quilt sandwich is ready for quilting. Quilting is the best part of the process for me. It wasn't always so, but I now think there can never be too much quilting on a project. Don't be discouraged if your first stitches seem a little long. If you start hand quilting in the middle of the quilt, by the time you reach the edges, they will be much smaller. For hand-quilting instructions, I recommend *Loving Stitches: A Guide to Fine Hand Quilting* by Jeana Kimball (That Patchwork Place, 1992), or you can take a hand-quilting class.

Machine quilting is also an option. It's suitable for all types of quilts, from wall hangings to crib quilts to full-size bed quilts. With machine quilting, you can quickly complete quilts that might otherwise languish on the shelves of your sewing room. The "Polka Dots!" quilt on page 32 was machine quilted, as was "Pathway to the Stars" on page 88.

Marking the quilting design is only necessary if you need to follow a grid or a complex pattern. It is not necessary if you plan to quilt in the ditch, outline quilt a uniform distance from seam lines, or free-motion quilt in a random pattern.

For straight-line quilting, it is extremely helpful to have a walking foot (built in or an attachment) to feed the quilt layers through the machine without shifting or puckering.

For free-motion quilting, you need a darning foot and the ability to drop or cover the feed dogs on your machine. With free-motion quilting, you guide the fabric in the direction of the design rather than turning the fabric under the needle. Use free-motion quilting to outline quilt a fabric motif or to create stippling or other curved designs.

For more specific information on machine quilting, I recommend *Machine Quilting Made Easy* by Maurine Noble (That Patchwork Place, 1994).

Binding

QUILT BINDING CAN be cut on the straight of grain or on the bias. I prefer bias binding because it wears better. As a rule, allow ½ yard of fabric to bind a crib quilt or wall hanging, ¾ yard for a twin-size quilt, 1 yard for a full- or queen-size bed quilt, and 1¼ yards for a king-size bed quilt.

1. Cut the binding fabric into 2½"-wide bias strips.

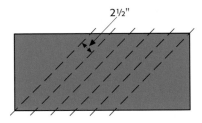

2. Sew the bias strips together end to end to make one long bias strip. Press the seams open.

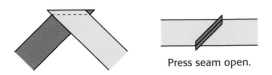

Press seam open.

3. Fold the strip in half lengthwise, wrong sides together, and press.

Fold line

4. Unfold one end of the binding and turn under the short edge ¼". Starting in the center on one side of the quilt, stitch the binding to the quilt with the raw edges of the binding even with the edges of the quilt top. Using a walking foot will help feed all layers of the quilt and binding through your machine evenly and prevent ripples. I use a ⅜" seam allowance. Stitch to within ⅜" of the corner. Backstitch and remove the quilt from the machine. Turn the top so you are ready to stitch the next side. To miter the corner, fold the binding up as shown to form a 45° angle.

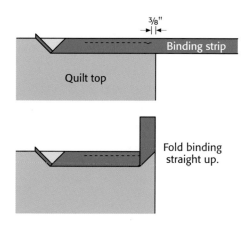
⅜"
Binding strip
Quilt top
Fold binding straight up.

5. Fold the binding down, keeping the fold even with the top edge of the quilt. Pin the pleat formed at the fold in place. Stitch, ending the stitching ⅜" from the next corner. Repeat the process for the remaining sides.

Begin sewing ⅜" from top edge.

6. When you reach the beginning of the binding, cut the binding 1" longer than needed and tuck

the end inside the beginning of the strip. Stitch the rest of the binding. Fold the binding over the raw edges of the quilt and blindstitch in place on the quilt back. The corners will automatically form miters as you turn them. Slipstitch the miters closed.

Sew down.
Quilt back

Hanging Sleeve

To MAKE DISPLAYING your small wall projects easier, you may want to add a hanging sleeve. This is a tube of fabric, sewn on the back of the quilt after it is quilted, which allows a rod or dowel to be inserted for hanging.

1. To make a permanent sleeve, cut a strip of backing fabric equal to the width of the quilt by twice the desired width of the sleeve, plus ½" for seam allowances.

2. Turn under the raw edges ¼" at both narrow ends of the strip. Fold again and stitch in place.

3. Fold the sleeve in half along the length, wrong sides together, and press.

4. Before binding the quilt, pin the sleeve to the back of the quilt with the raw edges even with the top edge of the quilt.

5. Apply the binding to the quilt as usual, which will secure the top of the sleeve to the quilt back.

6. Carefully sew the bottom edge of the sleeve to the back of the quilt, making sure not to let your stitches go all the way through to the front.

Pierre

"PIERRE" IS MADE of drunkard's squares that use only two fabrics each for a more traditional look. But the number of colors is where tradition stops and serendipity takes over. It became apparent soon after I started working that I would run out of my original background fabric. Rather than dash to the store for more, I looked through my stash and found a fabric a shade darker. I used the lighter fabric for the red four-patch units and the darker fabric for the green four-patch units, and was pleasantly surprised by the subtle checkerboard that appeared in the background when I alternated them according to my original quilt plan. Sometimes surprises can be wonderful—this unplanned fabric shortage created a great look that I hadn't expected.

Quilt Sizes

Finished size of squares	Finished size of quilt
2" x 2"	32" x 40"
3" x 3"	48" x 60" (shown)
4" x 4"	64" x 80"

Materials

Yardage is based on 42"-wide fabric.

Decide the size of square you want to make; then follow the yardage requirements listed for that size.

Fabric	2" squares	3" squares	4" squares
Red	¾ yd.	1 yd.	1½ yds.
Background A	1¼ yds.	1¾ yds.	2½ yds.
Yellow	1¼ yds.	1¼ yds.	2 yds.
Green	¾ yd.	1 yd.	1½ yds.
Background B	1¼ yds.	1¾ yds.	2½ yds.

Cutting Dimensions

CUT THE FABRICS as indicated in the chart below, according to the size of drunkard's square you've chosen. The numbers of each kind of piece to cut after this first cutting are given in the directions for each section of the quilt. (Cutting the pieces when needed will help you keep track of them.)

Size of finished squares	2" x 2"	3" x 3"	4" x 4"
Size to cut strips for 45° triangles	2" x 42"	2½" x 42"	3" x 42"
Size to cut rectangles for wings	1½" x 5"	2" x 6½"	2½" x 8"
Ruler mark for cutting wings	6"	5½"	5"
Ruler mark for first trim of squares	2"	2¾"	3½"
Ruler mark for second trim of squares	2½"	3½"	4½"
Size to cut corner squares	2½" x 2½"	3½" x 3½"	4½" x 4½"
Size to cut border rectangles	2½" x 4½"	3½" x 6½"	4½" x 8½"
Size to cut miter strips	2½" x 42"	3½" x 42"	4½" x 42"
Ruler mark for miter cuts	4¼"	6¼"	8¼"

Red Four-Patch Units

Cutting

From red: Cut 48 wing pairs.
From background A: Cut 48 wing pairs and
    48 triangle pairs.
From yellow: Cut 48 triangle pairs.

Assembly

1. Make the drunkard's squares as shown.

Make 48 each.

2. Assemble the red and yellow drunkard's squares into 24 four-patch units as shown. Press the seam allowances toward the yellow squares.

Make 24.

Green Four-Patch Units

Cutting

From green: Cut 48 wing pairs.
From background B: Cut 48 wing pairs
    and 48 triangle pairs.
From yellow: Cut 48 triangle pairs.

Assembly

1. Make the drunkard's squares as shown.

Make 48 each.

2. Assemble the green and yellow drunkard's squares into 24 four-patch units as shown. Press the seam allowances toward the yellow squares.

Make 24.

Pierre Blocks

1. To assemble the Pierre block, lay out 2 red four-patch units and 2 green four-patch units as shown. Be careful to orient each unit so as to make the circular design.

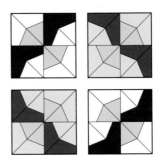

2. Stitch the four-patch units together to make the block. Press the seams toward the green four-patch units. Repeat to make 12 identical blocks.

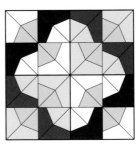

Make 12.

Row Assembly

THE QUILT IS constructed of two alternating rows, A and B.

1. For row A, lay out 3 Pierre blocks as shown, noting that the outer blocks have a red four-patch unit in the upper left corner and the center block has a green four-patch unit in the upper left corner.

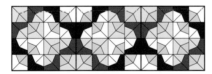

Row A
Make 2.

2. Sew the row A blocks together; press the seam allowances toward the right. Repeat to make a second row A.

3. For row B, lay out 3 Pierre blocks as shown, noting that the outer blocks have a green four-patch unit in the upper left corner and the center block has a red four-patch unit in the upper left corner.

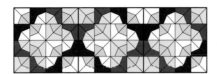

Row B
Make 2.

4. Sew the row B blocks together; press the seam allowances toward the left. Repeat to make a second row B.

5. Sew the rows together, alternating row A and row B as shown, to complete the center of the quilt top.

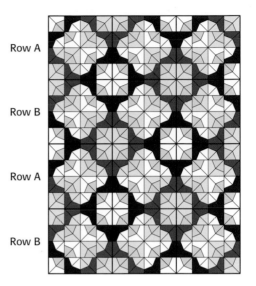

Row A

Row B

Row A

Row B

Inner Border

Cutting

From background A: Cut 14 wing pairs, 2 triangle pairs, 4 corner squares, and 5 border rectangles.
From background B: Cut 14 wing pairs, 2 triangle pairs, 4 corner squares, and 5 border rectangles.
From yellow: Cut 28 triangle pairs.
From red: Cut 2 wing pairs.
From green: Cut 2 wing pairs.

Assembly

1. Make the drunkard's squares as shown.

Make 14 each.   Make 2 each.

2. Sew the yellow drunkard's squares together in pairs to make arches. Half the units should have background A fabric on the right and background B fabric on the left, and the other half should be reversed.

Make 7 each.

3. Lay out the drunkard's squares, corner squares, and border rectangles for the right inner border as shown. Sew the units together; then sew the border to the right side of the quilt (do this now so you won't confuse it with the other inner borders, which aren't exactly the same). Attach the border with the yellow triangles facing toward the quilt center.

Right Inner Border

4. Lay out the units for the left inner border as shown. Sew the units together; then sew the border to the left side of the quilt, with the yellow triangles facing toward the quilt center.

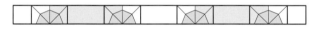

Left Inner Border

5. Lay out the units for the top and bottom inner borders as shown. Sew the units together. (Notice that they aren't identical, but are mirror images.) Sew the borders to the quilt, with the yellow triangles facing toward the quilt center.

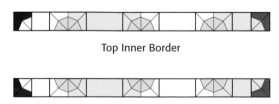

Top Inner Border

Bottom Inner Border

Outer Border

Cutting

From background A: Cut 14 triangle pairs.
From background B: Cut 14 triangle pairs.
From red: Cut 14 wing pairs, 5 border rectangles, and 1 strip for miter pieces.
From green: Cut 14 wing pairs, 5 border rectangles, and 1 strip for miter pieces.

Assembly

1. Make the drunkard's squares for the outer border as shown.

Make 14 each.

2. Sew the red and green drunkard's squares together in pairs to form arches, half with green wings on the left and half with green wings on the right, as shown.

Make 7 each.

3. Using the red and green miter strips, cut the pieces needed for the mitered corners. Use the ruler mark for miter cuts in "Cutting Dimensions" on page 21 to cut the length needed for the size of squares you're working with. The same measurement is used for all 8 miter pieces.

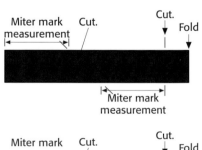

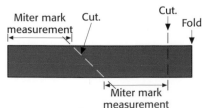

4. Lay out the miter corners, the arches, and the border rectangles for the top outer border as shown. Sew the pieces together; then attach the border to the quilt. Begin and end the seam ¼" from the mitered edges. Note: the quilt top will extend ¼" beyond the borders at both ends.

Top Outer Border

5. In the same manner, lay out and piece the right outer border. Sew it to the right side of the quilt. Start sewing ¼" from the top end of the quilt where the seam for the top border ended. Stop sewing ¼" from the other end.

Right Outer Border

6. In the same manner, lay out and piece the bottom outer border. Sew it to the bottom of the quilt top.

Bottom Outer Border

7. Repeat for left outer border.

Left Outer Border

8. Referring to "Adding Mitered Borders" on page 16, finish the miter corners.

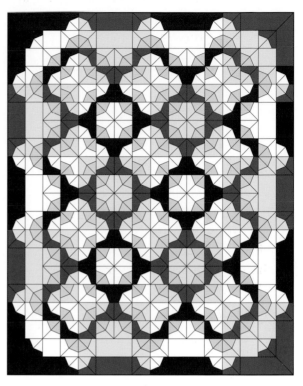

Quilt Plan

Finishing

LAYER AND BASTE your quilt top; then quilt by hand or machine. For specific details on quilting and binding, see "Techniques for Finishing," starting on page 16. You may also want to add a hanging sleeve and label to your quilt.

Renaissance

By Mary Sue Suit, 60" x 76"

This handsome quilt may look complex and quite scrappy, but it's really much simpler than that. The X and the O blocks use identical four-patch units; they're just rotated differently.

Even the scrappy look is planned. This quilt is made using four color values: light, medium, medium-dark, and dark. I used a single muslin throughout for the lights, and chose golds for the mediums, rusts for the medium-darks, and dark browns for the darks. You can use one fabric for each value, or select eight different ones as I did for a dynamic, scrappy look. You can even change the color scheme entirely. Just follow the value placements and use your favorite colors. Each set of fabrics will work together differently, so choose the outer border fabric after you've completed the center of the quilt.

Quilt Sizes

Finished size of squares	Finished size of quilt
2" x 2"	30" x 38"
3" x 3"	45" x 57"
4" x 4"	60" x 76" (shown)

Materials

Yardage is based on 42"-wide fabric.

Decide the size of square you want to make; then follow the yardage requirements listed for that size.

Fabric	2" squares	3" squares	4" squares
Medium-dark	¾ yd.	1 yd.	1¼ yds.
OR 2 strips *each* of 8 different fabrics	1½" x 42"	2" x 42"	2½" x 42"
Medium	½ yd.	¾ yd.	¾ yd.
OR 1 strip *each* of 8 different fabrics	2" x 42"	2½" x 42"	3" x 42"
Muslin	1¼ yds.	1½ yds.	1¾ yds.
Dark	½ yd.	¾ yd.	¾ yd.
OR 1 strip *each* of 8 different fabrics	2" x 42"	2½" x 42"	3" x 42"
Medium-scale print	¼ yd.	½ yd.	½ yd.
Large-scale print	¼ yd.	½ yd.	½ yd.
Print for outer border	⅓ yd.	¾ yd.	1¼ yds.
Backing	1¼ yds.	2⅞ yds.	3½ yds.
Binding	½ yd.	¾ yd.	1 yd.
Batting	34" x 42"	49" x 61"	64" x 80"

Cutting Dimensions

Cut the fabrics as indicated in the chart below, according to the size of drunkard's square you've chosen. The numbers of each kind of piece to cut after this first cutting are given in the directions for each section of the quilt. (Cutting the pieces when needed will help you keep track of them.)

Size of finished squares	2" x 2"	3" x 3"	4" x 4"
Size to cut strips for 45° triangles	2" x 42"	2½" x 42"	3" x 42"
Size to cut rectangles for wings	1½" x 5"	2" x 6½"	2½" x 8"
Ruler mark for cutting wings	6"	5½"	5"
Ruler mark for first trim of squares	2"	2¾"	3½"
Ruler mark for second trim of squares	2½"	3½"	4½"

X and O Blocks

Cutting

From medium-dark: Cut 64 wing pairs (8 pairs each from 8 different fabrics).

From medium: Cut 64 triangle pairs (8 pairs each from 8 different fabrics).

From muslin: Cut 64 wing pairs.

From dark: Cut 64 triangle pairs (8 pairs each from 8 different fabrics).

Assembly

1. Make the drunkard's squares as shown. For the medium-and-medium-dark drunkard's squares, press the right wing seam allowances toward the medium fabric and the left wing seam allowances toward the medium-dark fabric for easier seam matching. For the muslin-and-dark squares, press all seam allowances toward the dark fabric to prevent show-through.

Make 64 each.

2. Arrange 2 muslin-and-dark drunkard's squares with 2 medium-and-medium-dark drunkard's squares to make a four-patch unit. Make sure the medium-dark wings point toward the center of the block and the muslin wings point toward the outer corners. Stitch the four-patch unit together. Press pairs toward the medium-dark fabric to butt center seam. Repeat to make 32 four-patch units.

Make 32.

3. Lay out 4 four-patch units to make an X block as shown. In each quadrant, the medium triangles should point toward the center of the block and toward the 4 corners. Stitch the units together and press the seams. Repeat to make 6 X blocks.

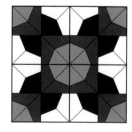

X Block
Make 6.

4. Lay out 4 four-patch units to make an O block as shown. In each quadrant, the muslin wings should point toward the center of the block and toward the 4 corners. Stitch the units together and press the seams. Repeat to make 2 O blocks.

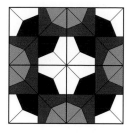

O Block
Make 2.

5. Lay out 2 rows of 3 blocks each, as shown. The X blocks are on the outside and the O blocks are in the centers. Stitch the blocks together and press the seam allowances toward the right in one row and toward the left in the other.

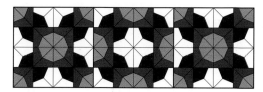

Make 2.

6. Sew the rows together.

Corner Block Assembly

THE CORNERS OF the quilt are made from a large-scale print, with mitered corners in a second print.

Cutting Dimensions

Size of finished squares	2" x 2"	3" x 3"	4" x 4"
Size to cut medium-scale print	4½" x 42"	6½" x 42"	8½" x 42"
Ruler mark for miter cut of medium-scale print	2¼"	3¼"	4¼"
Size to cut large-scale print	2½" x 42"	3½" x 42"	4½" x 42"
Ruler mark for miter cut of large-scale print	6¼"	9¼"	12¼"

Cutting

From medium-scale print: Cut miter strips (one 2½", two 3½", or four 4½" strips, depending on the size of blocks you are making) and 4 triangle pairs.

From large-scale print: Cut 4 pairs of miter strips.

From muslin: Cut 4 wing pairs.

Assembly

1. Make 4 drunkard's squares as shown.

Make 4.

2. Cut miter strips from the large-scale print using the miter mark listed for the size of quilt you are making in "Cutting Dimensions" above.

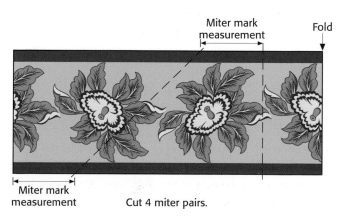

Miter mark measurement

Fold

Miter mark measurement

Cut 4 miter pairs.

3. Sew the large-scale miter strips to the drunkard's squares as shown. Press the seam allowances toward one side.

Make 4.

4. Cut miter strips from the medium-scale print, using the miter mark listed for the size of quilt you are making in "Cutting Dimensions" on page 29.

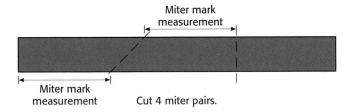

Miter mark measurement

Miter mark measurement   Cut 4 miter pairs.

5. Sew the medium-scale print miter sections to the corner units made in step 3 to complete 4 corner blocks. Press.

Make 4 corner blocks.

6. Stitch a corner block to each side of an X block as shown. Repeat to make a second identical row.

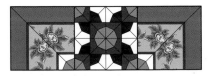

Make 2 rows.

7. Stitch the corner-block rows to the top and bottom of the quilt, referring to the quilt plan on page 31.

Mom's Flannel Fun

DESIGNED AND PIECED
BY MARY LUCAS,
MACHINE QUILTED BY KATHY BARNES,
60" x 76"

SURPRISE! THIS COZY flannel lap quilt was made using the same basic quilt design as my "Renaissance" quilt. The look is completely different because Mary used fewer fabrics and changed the placement of the color values. This cheery quilt is a wonderful example of what you can create by using your own interpretation of the pattern provided.

Borders

THIS QUILT HAS a muslin inner border cut on the lengthwise grain, and an outer border cut on the crosswise grain and pieced to the length needed. The cutting dimensions for each size of quilt are given below.

Border Cutting

Size of finished squares	2" x 2"	3" x 3"	4" x 4"
Top and bottom inner borders Cut 2 strips	1½" x 28"	2" x 41"	2½" x 54"
Side inner borders Cut 2 strips	1½" x 36"	2" x 53"	2½" x 70"
Ruler mark for inner-border miter cuts Top and bottom borders Side borders	24" 32"	36" 48"	48" 64"
Top and bottom outer borders Cut 2 strips	2½" x 32"	3½" x 47"	4½" x 62"
Side outer borders Cut 2 strips	2½" x 40"	3½" x 59"	4½" x 78"
Ruler mark for outer-border miter cuts Top and bottom borders Side borders	26" 34"	39" 51"	52" 68"

Assembly

1. Cut the inner borders according to "Border Cutting" above. Sew them to the quilt top, referring to "Adding Mitered Borders" on page 00 for details.

2. Cut the outer borders according to "Border Cutting" above. For the larger quilts, you will need to sew 2 strips together to get the length needed. Sew the outer borders to the quilt top.

Finishing

LAYER AND BASTE your quilt top; then quilt by hand or machine. For specific details on quilting and binding, see "Techniques for Finishing," starting on page 16. You may also want to add a hanging sleeve and label to your quilt.

Quilt Plan

Polka Dots!

By Mary Sue Suit, 48" x 56". Machine quilted by Judy Woodworth.

OVER THE YEARS I have noticed that I have two distinct trends in fabric buying. First, I like fabric with large polka dots, but seldom purchase it because I have a hard time working with it. Second, I have no problem buying fabrics with large, unusual prints, even though I have no clue how I will use them. "Polka Dots!" became the solution to my large-print dilemma. I made polka-dot designs with the piecing and let the large-scale print fall where it might.

In this case I took my color cues for the polka dots from a large-scale print fabric with a black background. Since I hate to fussy cut I just attacked the print with gusto and let it recombine randomly as the squares were pieced. I love the final result because I never see the same quilt twice. Each time I look at it, I catch an unexpected glimpse of the main print.

Just make sure you use fabrics with small-scale prints that read as solid for the polka dots, or they will become lost in the large-print background. Don't be afraid to be bold and have fun.

Quilt Sizes

Finished size of squares	Finished size of quilt
2" x 2"	24" x 28"
3" x 3"	36" x 42"
4" x 4"	48" x 56" (shown)

Materials

Yardage is based on 42"-wide fabric.

Decide the size of square you want to make; then follow the yardage requirements listed for that size.

Fabric	2" squares	3" squares	4" squares
Light background	¼ yd.	¼ yd.	¼ yd.
Medium background	⅓ yd.	½ yd.	½ yd.
Large-scale print	1 yd.	1½ yds.	2 yds.
Medium-dark background	⅓ yd.	½ yd.	¾ yd.
Lavender	¼ yd.	¼ yd.	⅓ yd.
Red	¼ yd.	⅓ yd.	½ yd.
Green	¼ yd.	¼ yd.	⅓ yd.
Backing	1 yd.	1⅜ yds.	2⅞ yds.
Binding	½ yd.	¾ yd.	1 yd.
Batting	28" x 32"	40" x 46"	52" x 60"

Cutting Dimensions

CUT THE FABRICS as indicated in the chart below, according to the size of drunkard's square you've chosen. The numbers of each kind of piece to cut after this first cutting are given in the directions for each section of the quilt. (Cutting the pieces when needed will help you keep track of them.)

Size of finished squares	2" x 2"	3" x 3"	4" x 4"
Size to cut strips for 45° triangles	2" x 42"	2½" x 42"	3" x 42"
Size to cut rectangles for wings	1½" x 5"	2" x 6½"	2½" x 8"
Ruler mark for cutting wings	6"	5½"	5"
Ruler mark for first trim of squares	2"	2¾"	3½"
Ruler mark for second trim of squares	2½"	3½"	4½"

Center Blocks

Cutting

From light background: Cut 14 wing pairs.
From medium background: Cut 10 wing pairs.
From large-scale print: Cut 24 triangle pairs.

Assembly

1. Make 24 drunkard's squares as shown.

Make 8.   Make 6 each.   Make 4.

2. Lay out the drunkard's squares to make 4 blocks with half medium background and half light background, as shown. Stitch the blocks.

Make 4.

3. Make 2 more center blocks, but this time, only 2 medium-background wings are used in each. Stitch the blocks.

Make 2.

4. Assemble the center section of the quilt by stitching the 6 blocks together as shown.

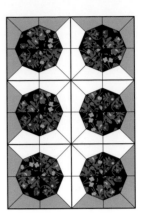

First Border

Cutting

From medium-dark background: Cut 4 wing pairs.
From large-scale print: Cut 20 wing pairs and
    4 triangle pairs.
From medium background: Cut 20 triangle pairs.

Assembly

1. Make the drunkard's squares as shown.

Make 4.   Make 20.

2. Sew the 20 medium-background-and-large-scale-print drunkard's squares together in pairs to make arch units.

Make 10.

3. Sew 3 arch units together to make a side border. Repeat to make another side border. Sew the remaining arch pairs together in pairs (2 arches each) and sew a medium-dark-background-and-large-scale-print drunkard's square to each end to make a top and a bottom border.

Side Border
Make 2.

Top and Bottom Border
Make 2.

4. Sew the side borders to the quilt center. Press seams toward the quilt center. Add the top and bottom sections to the quilt center and press the seam allowances toward the quilt center.

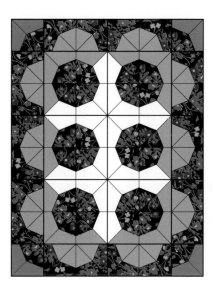

Second Border

COLORFUL POLKA DOTS make up the next round. I recommend making all the Polka Dot blocks of one color at the same time to avoid confusion with the wing pieces.

Lavender Polka Dot Blocks

CUTTING
From medium-dark background: Cut 8 wing pairs.
From large-scale print: Cut 8 wing pairs.
From lavender: Cut 16 triangle pairs.

ASSEMBLY
1. Make 4 drunkard's squares in each of the 4 color combinations, as shown.

Make 4 each.

2. Sew the drunkard's squares together as shown to make 4 lavender Polka Dot blocks.

Make 4.

Red Polka Dot Blocks

CUTTING
From medium-dark background: Cut 16 wing pairs.
From large-scale print: Cut 16 wing pairs.
From red: Cut 32 triangle pairs.

ASSEMBLY
1. Make 8 drunkard's squares in each of the 4 color combinations, as shown.

Make 8 each.

2. Sew the drunkard's squares together as shown to make 4 of each type of red Polka Dot block, which are mirror images of each other. Make sure the color placement matches that in the diagram.

Make 4 each.

Green Polka Dot Blocks

CUTTING

From medium-dark background: Cut 6 wing pairs.
From large-scale print: Cut 18 wing pairs.
From green: Cut 24 triangle pairs.

ASSEMBLY

1. Make the drunkard's squares as shown.

Make 6 each.   Make 12.

2. Sew the drunkard's squares together as shown to make 6 green Polka Dot blocks. Make sure the color placement matches that in the diagram.

Make 6.

Assembling the Second Border

1. Using the red and green Polka Dot blocks, make 2 side borders, as shown, paying careful attention to color placement.

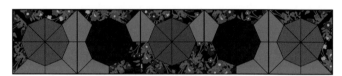

Side Border
Make 2.

2. Sew the side borders to the quilt so the medium-dark-background wings point toward the outer edges of the quilt.

3. Using the lavender and remaining red and green Polka Dot blocks, make a top and a bottom border, referring to the diagram for color placement.

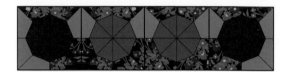

Top and Bottom Border
Make 2.

4. Sew the top and bottom borders to the quilt so the medium-dark-background wings point toward the outer edges of the quilt.

Third Border

This quilt has a third border that is cut from the large-scale print on the crossgrain and pieced to the length needed. The cutting dimensions for each size of quilt are given below.

Border Cutting

Size of finished squares	2" x 2"	3" x 3"	4" x 4"
Size to cut top and bottom borders Cut 2 strips	2½" x 26"	3½" x 38"	4½" x 50"
Size to cut side borders Cut 2 strips	2½" x 30"	3½" x 44"	4½" x 58"
Ruler mark for miter cuts Top and bottom borders Side borders	20" 24"	30" 36"	40" 48"

Assembly

Cut the borders according to "Border Cutting" above. Sew them to the quilt top, referring to the quilt plan at right and "Adding Mitered Borders" on page 16 for details.

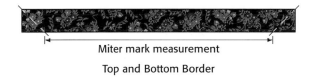

Miter mark measurement

Top and Bottom Border

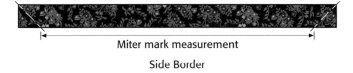

Miter mark measurement

Side Border

Finishing

Layer and baste your quilt top; then quilt by hand or machine. For specific details on quilting and binding, see "Techniques for Finishing," starting on page 16. You may also want to add a hanging sleeve and label to your quilt.

Quilt Plan

Burgundy Garden

BY MARY SUE SUIT, 64" x 80". MACHINE QUILTED BY JUDY WOODWORTH.

My ORIGINAL IDEA for this quilt was quite different from the finished project you see here. My plan wasn't quite working out the way I had hoped, but after investing so much time and fabric in the project, I felt the need to keep going. I changed a few things and kept twisting and turning the blocks until I finally found a path I liked.

The four-patch configuration is the same throughout the quilt; only the colors within the four-patch units are changed. The tricky part about this quilt is keeping the two gold and two light-background fabrics straight. Their subtle differences add depth to the quilt, so it's worth the extra attention it takes to be sure you're always cutting with the gold A fabric on top!

As a final design statement, I used drunkard's squares with gold wings as border corners and continued that burst of color around the quilt with the gold binding. Binding is often overlooked, but see what an effective design element it can be.

Quilt Sizes

Finished size of squares	Finished size of quilt
2" x 2"	32" x 40"
3" x 3"	48" x 60"
4" x 4"	64" x 80" (shown)

Materials

Yardage is based on 42"-wide fabric.

Decide the size of square you want to make; then follow the yardage requirements listed for that size.

Fabric	2" squares	3" squares	4" squares
Burgundy A	1 yd.	1½ yds.	2 yds.
Gold A	½ yd.	⅔ yd.	¾ yd.
Gold B (includes binding)	1½ yds.	1⅔ yds.	2 yds.
Background A	½ yd.	¾ yd.	1 yd.
Background B	½ yd.	¾ yd.	1 yd.
Pink print	¾ yd.	1 yd.	1¼ yds.
Blue print	¾ yd.	1 yd.	1¼ yds.
Burgundy B	1 yd.	1½ yds.	1¾ yds.
Backing	1⅜ yds.	2⅞ yds.	4⅔ yds.
Batting	36" x 44"	52" x 64"	68" x 84"

Cutting Dimensions

CUT THE FABRICS as indicated in the chart below, according to the size of drunkard's square you've chosen. The numbers of each kind of piece to cut after this first cutting are given in the directions for each section of the quilt. (Cutting the pieces when needed will help you keep track of them.)

Size of finished squares	2" x 2"	3" x 3"	4" x 4"
Size to cut strips for 45° triangles	2" x 42"	2½" x 42"	3" x 42"
Size to cut rectangles for wings	1½" x 5"	2" x 6½"	2½" x 8"
Ruler mark for cutting wings	6"	5½"	5"
Ruler mark for first trim of squares	2"	2¾"	3½"
Ruler mark for second trim of squares	2½"	3½"	4½"
Size to cut plain squares	2½" x 2½"	3½" x 3½"	4½" x 4½"

Pink Four-Patch Units

Cutting

From burgundy A: Cut 60 wing pairs.

From gold A and gold B, layered wrong sides together and with gold A on top: Cut 24 wing pairs.

From background A and background B, layered wrong sides together and with background A on top: Cut 12 wing pairs.

From pink print: Cut 96 triangle pairs.

Assembly

1. Make the drunkard's squares as shown.

Make 36.   Make 24 each.   Make 12.

2. Make 12 pink four-patch units as shown, carefully following the color placement. (These four-patch units only use half of the drunkard's squares you have made. Don't use them all!)

Make 12.

3. Make 12 more pink four-patch units as shown. This time, use the drunkard's squares with the background wings in the top left corner.

Make 12.

Blue Four-Patch Units

Cutting

From burgundy A: Cut 36 wing pairs.

From gold A and gold B, layered wrong sides together and with gold A on top: Cut 12 wing pairs.

From blue print: Cut 48 triangle pairs.

Assembly

1. Make the drunkard's squares as shown.

Make 24.   Make 12 each.

2. Make 12 blue four-patch units as shown, carefully following the color placement.

Make 12.

Blue-and-Background Four-Patch Units

Cutting

From burgundy A: Cut 24 wing pairs.

From gold A and gold B, layered wrong sides together and with gold A on top: Cut 12 wing pairs.

From background A and background B, layered wrong sides together and with background A on top: Cut 12 wing pairs.

From blue print: Cut 48 triangle pairs.

Assembly

1. Make the drunkard's squares as shown.

Make 12 each.

2. Make 12 four-patch units as shown, carefully following the color placement.

Make 12.

Block Assembly

1. Alternating the pink and blue four-patch units, lay out and piece 2 A blocks as shown. Pay careful attention to the color placement and orientation of each four-patch unit.

 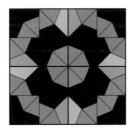

Block A
Make 2.

2. Using units from each group of four-patch units, make blocks B–E as shown. The blocks look very similar, so pay careful attention to the color placement. Label each stack of blocks, as they're easy to confuse.

  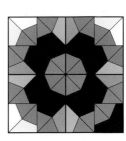

Block B
Make 2.

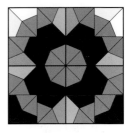

Block C
Make 2.

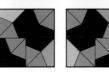 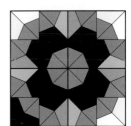

Block D
Make 2.

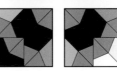  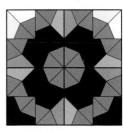

Block E
Make 4.

Quilt Assembly

The quilt is made of 2 alternating rows. Each row has 3 blocks.

1. Lay out 2 rows with block A in the center and a block E on either side. Note that the E blocks are rotated so that the burgundy wing corners face block A on both sides and the background wing corners face the edges of the quilt top. Double-check the block position and sew the blocks into rows. These are the 2 center rows of the quilt.

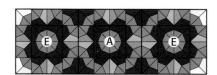

Center Row
Make 2.

2. Lay out 2 rows with block B on the left, block C in the center, and block D on the right. Double-check the block positions and sew the blocks into rows. These are the top and bottom rows.

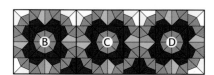

Top and Bottom Row
Make 2.

3. Sew the rows together to make the quilt center, taking care to position the rows correctly. The B-C-D rows are on the top and bottom of the quilt, each with the background wing corners facing toward the edges of the quilt.

Inner Border

Cutting

From burgundy B: Cut 18 wing pairs.

From background A and background B, layered wrong sides together and with background A on top: Cut 4 triangle pairs, 14 wing pairs, and 14 squares of each.

From blue print: Cut 8 triangle pairs.

From pink print: Cut 8 triangle pairs.

From gold A and gold B, layered wrong sides together and with gold A on top: Cut 14 triangle pairs.

Assembly

1. Make the drunkard's squares as shown.

Make 4.   Make 8 each.

2. Sew the drunkard's squares together in pairs to make 8 arch units.

Make 8.

3. Using the arch units and plain squares, lay out and piece 2 side inner borders as shown.

Side Border
Make 2.

4. Sew the side inner borders to the quilt top, referring to the quilt plan at right.

5. Make the drunkard's squares as shown; then sew them together in pairs to make 6 arch units.

Make 6 each.   Make 6.

6. Using the arch units and plain squares, lay out and piece the top and bottom inner borders. Sew the borders to the quilt top, referring to the quilt plan.

Top and Bottom Border
Make 2.

Outer Border

Cutting Dimensions

Size of finished squares	2" x 2"	3" x 3"	4" x 4"
Size to cut side borders	2½" x 36½"	3½" x 54½"	4½" x 72"
Size to cut top and bottom borders	2½" x 28½"	3½" x 42½"	4½" x 56½"

Cutting

From burgundy B: Cut 4 triangle pairs, 2 side borders, and a top and a bottom border.
From gold A: Cut 4 wing pairs.

Assembly

1. Make the drunkard's squares as shown.

Make 4.

2. Sew the side outer borders to the quilt top.

3. Sew a drunkard's square to each end of the top and bottom outer borders.

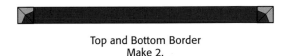

Top and Bottom Border
Make 2.

4. Sew the top and bottom outer borders to the quilt.

Quilt Plan

Finishing

LAYER AND BASTE your quilt top; then quilt by hand or machine. For specific details on quilting and binding, see "Techniques for Finishing," starting on page 16. You may also want to add a hanging sleeve and label to your quilt.

Twirly Mae

By Mary Sue Suit, 26" x 26"

The Twirly Mae block features motion galore. Splitting the drunkard's square into four pieces lets you create a spinning pinwheel. The trick is to get all the fabrics in the correct places; when you do, the result is quite exciting. Vivid batiks set against white add to the liveliness, and easy-to-piece sashing connects the path for fun and adventure. The drunkard's squares used for the border corners give a rounded illusion, and the binding, as in "Burgundy Garden" (page 38), makes a final color statement on this spunky little quilt.

While the quilt shown is quite small, you can easily enlarge it either by starting with larger drunkard's squares or by adding more rows of blocks and sashing strips. You won't believe how easy it is.

Quilt Sizes

Finished size of squares	Finished size of quilt
2" x 2"	26" x 26" (shown)
3" x 3"	39" x 39"
4" x 4"	52" x 52"

Materials

Yardage is based on 42"-wide fabric.

Decide the size of square you want to make; then follow the yardage requirements listed for that size.

Fabric	2" squares	3" squares	4" squares
White	½ yd.	¾ yd.	1 yd.
Blue	½ yd.	¾ yd.	1 yd.
Yellow	¾ yd.	1 yd.	1¼ yds.
Orange	¾ yd.	1 yd.	1 yd.

Cutting Dimensions

Cut the fabrics as indicated in the chart below, according to the size of drunkard's square you've chosen. The numbers of each kind of piece to cut after this first cutting are given in the directions for each section of the quilt. (Cutting the pieces when needed will help you keep track of them.)

Size of finished squares	2" x 2"	3" x 3"	4" x 4"
Size to cut strips for 45° triangles	2" x 42"	2½" x 42"	3" x 42"
Size to cut rectangles for wings	1½" x 5"	2" x 6½"	2½" x 8"
Ruler mark for cutting wings	6"	5½"	5"
Ruler mark for first trim of squares	2"	2¾"	3½"
Ruler mark for second trim of squares	2½"	3½"	4½"
Size to cut rectangles for sashing	2½" x 4½"	3½" x 6½"	4½" x 8½"
Size to cut center squares	2½" x 2½"	3½" x 3½"	4½" x 4½"
Size to cut strips for inner borders	2½" x 18½"	3½" x 27½"	4½" x 36½"
Size to cut strips for outer borders	2½" x 22½"	3½" x 33½"	4½" x 44½"

Twirly Mae Blocks

Cutting

From white: Cut 32 wing pairs.

From blue: Cut 16 wing pairs.

From blue and yellow, layered wrong sides together and with blue on top: Cut 16 wing pairs.

From orange: Cut 32 triangle pairs.

From yellow: Cut 16 triangle pairs.

From yellow and orange, layered wrong sides together and with yellow on top: Cut 16 triangle pairs.

Assembly

1. Make the drunkard's squares as shown.

Make 16 each.

2. Using 1 of each color combination of drunkard's squares per unit, make 16 four-patch units. Be careful to orient the squares exactly as shown.

Make 16.

3. Rotate the four-patch units to make 4 Twirly Mae blocks as shown.

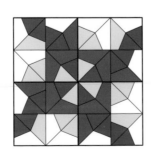

Twirly Mae Block
Make 4.

Sashing and Borders

The sashing is assembled from drunkard's squares, rectangles, and center squares. See "Cutting Dimensions" on page 45 for the appropriate sizes to cut the rectangles and the inner and outer borders.

Cutting

From white: Cut 4 sashing rectangles and 8 wing pairs.

From orange: Cut 12 triangle pairs.

From yellow: Cut 1 center square, 4 wing pairs, and 4 triangle pairs.

From blue: Cut 4 triangle pairs.

Assembly

1. Make the drunkard's squares as shown. The orange-and-yellow drunkard's squares are used in the border corners. Set them aside.

Make 8.   Make 4 each.

2. Make 4 sashing strips by stitching a white-and-orange drunkard's square to each end of a white rectangle. Be sure to position the drunkard's squares as shown.

Sashing Strip
Make 4.

3. Lay out the Twirly Mae blocks, sashing strips, and center squares as shown. Sew the units together in rows; then sew the rows together.

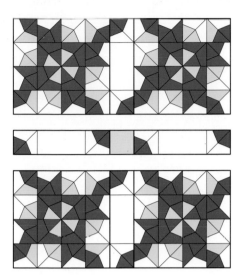

4. Sew the orange inner borders to the sides of the quilt top. Press the seam allowances toward the orange fabric.

5. Sew a yellow-and-orange drunkard's square to both ends of the orange top and bottom inner borders. Press the seam allowances toward the borders; then sew the borders to the quilt top with the yellow wings pointing toward the outer corners.

Top and Bottom Inner Border
Make 2.

6. Sew the yellow outer borders to the sides of the quilt top. Press the seam allowances toward the outer borders.

7. Sew a blue-and-yellow drunkard's square to both ends of the yellow top and bottom outer borders. Press the seam allowances toward the center; then, referring to the quilt plan, sew the borders to the quilt top with the blue wings pointing toward the outer corners.

Top and Bottom Outer Border
Make 2.

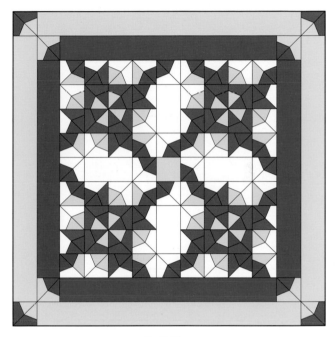

Quilt Plan

Finishing

LAYER AND BASTE your quilt top; then quilt by hand or machine. For specific details on quilting and binding, see "Techniques for Finishing," starting on page 16. You may also want to add a hanging sleeve and label to your quilt.

Stars in the Night Sky

BY MARY SUE SUIT, 30" x 36"

Using half-drunkard's squares, it's possible to piece blocks that look just like twinkling stars. This design incorporates, in addition to the yellow and gold star fabrics, seven different blue fabrics ranging from light to bright to very dark.

Whether you rummage through your stash and fat-quarter collection or buy new fabrics for this project, the best way to organize your cutting is to number your blue fabrics from one to seven. Blue 1, 4, and 7 are background fabrics and are cut by themselves. The others are cut in pairs. Layer the pairs of blue fabrics wrong sides together, with the lower number on top for cutting. Then twist and turn the pieced squares to let the colors flow. Changing color values across the quilt top make the design sparkle.

Materials

Yardage is based on 42"-wide fabric.

Decide the size of square you want to make; then follow the yardage requirements listed for that size.

Fabric	2" squares	3" squares	4" squares
White	3/8 yd.	1/4 yd.	1/4 yd.
Yellow	1/4 yd.	1/4 yd.	1/2 yd.
Gold	1/4 yd.	1/4 yd.	1/2 yd.
Blue 1 (light)	1/2 yd.	1/2 yd.	3/4 yd.
Blue 2 (medium light)	1/4 yd.	1/4 yd.	1/4 yd.
Blue 3 (bright)	1/4 yd.	1/4 yd.	1/4 yd.
Blue 4 (mottled royal)	1/4 yd.	1/3 yd.	1/2 yd.
Blue 5 (dark)	1/4 yd.	1/4 yd.	1/4 yd.
Blue 6 (dark)	1/4 yd.	1/4 yd.	1/4 yd.
Blue 7 (dark; includes binding)	1/2 yd.	3/4 yd.	1 yd.
Backing	3/4 yd.	1 yd.	2 1/2 yds.
Batting	24" x 28"	34" x 40"	44" x 52"

Quilt Sizes

Finished size of squares	Finished size of quilt
2" x 2"	20" x 24"
3" x 3"	30" x 36" (shown)
4" x 4"	40" x 48"

Cutting Dimensions

Cut the fabrics as indicated in the chart below, according to the size of drunkard's square you've chosen. The numbers of each kind of piece to cut after this first cutting are given in the directions for each section of the quilt. (Cutting the pieces when needed will help you keep track of them.)

Size of finished squares	2" x 2"	3" x 3"	4" x 4"
Size to cut strips for 45° triangles	2" x 42"	2½" x 42"	3" x 42"
Size to cut rectangles for wings	1½" x 5"	2" x 6½"	2½" x 8"
Ruler mark for cutting wings	6"	5½"	5"
Ruler mark for first trim of squares	2"	2¾"	3½"
Ruler mark for second trim of squares	2½"	3½"	4½"
Size to cut squares for half–drunkard's squares (cut in half diagonally)	3⅛" x 3⅛"	4⅛" x 4⅛"	5⅛" x 5⅛"
Size to cut plain squares	2½" x 2½"	3½" x 3½"	4½" x 4½"
Size to cut short border rectangles	2½" x 4½"	3½" x 6½"	4½" x 8½"
Size to cut long border rectangles	2½" x 8½"	3½" x 12½"	4½" x 16½"

Center Star Block

Cutting

From white: Cut 4 large squares and 4 triangle pairs.

From yellow: Cut 8 wing pairs.

From gold: Cut 8 triangle pairs.

From blue 2 and blue 3, layered wrong sides together and with blue 2 on top: Cut 4 wing pairs.

Assembly

1. Make the drunkard's squares as shown. Also make the half–drunkard's squares shown, 4 with left wings and triangles and 4 with right wings and triangles.

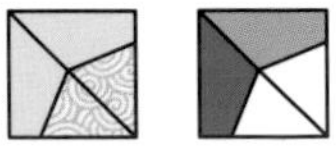

Drunkard's Square
Make 4 each.

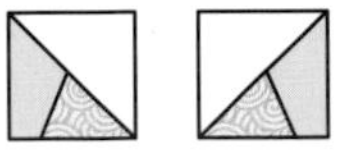

Half–Drunkard's Square
Make 4 each.

2. Lay out 1 of each of the drunkard's squares and half–drunkard's squares as shown to make a four-patch unit. Sew the four-patch unit together; then repeat to make a total of 4 four-patch units.

Make 4.

3. Lay out the four-patch units as shown, rotating them to form the Star block. Sew the four-patch units together to complete the block.

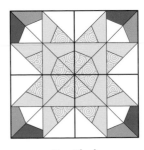

Star Block
Make 1.

Inner Round

The four-patch units that surround the Star block are made of drunkard's squares in three different colorways. You can cut everything all at once, or you can cut the pieces needed for one colorway at a time to prevent confusion. Be sure to label each of your blue fabrics by number to make things clearer.

Cutting

From blue 1: Cut 16 wing pairs and 8 triangle pairs.
From blue 2 and blue 3, layered wrong sides together and with blue 2 on top: Cut 8 wing pairs.
From blue 4: Cut 12 triangle pairs, 4 wing pairs, and 4 small plain.
From blue 5 and blue 6, layered wrong sides together and with blue 5 on top: Cut 16 triangle pairs and 12 wing pairs.
From gold: Cut 4 triangle pairs.

Fabric Color Key

- Blue 1
- Blue 2
- Blue 3
- Blue 4
- Blue 5
- Blue 6
- Blue 7

Assembly

1. Make the drunkard's squares as shown, carefully following the color placement.

Make 8 each.   Make 16.

2. Using the 3 different colorways, lay out a four-patch unit as shown. Sew the four-patch unit together; then repeat to make a total of 8 identical four-patch units. Note that you will have 4 extra of the drunkard's squares with blue 4 triangles; set these aside.

Make 8.

3. Sew the four-patch units together in pairs, placing them as shown.

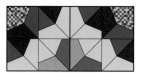

Make 4.

4. Sew 2 of the units to each side of the Star block as shown. Set aside the remaining units.

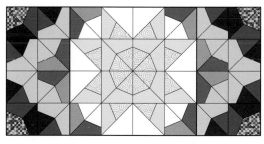

Center Row

5. Make the drunkard's squares as shown. Using these drunkard's squares, the leftover blue drunkard's squares from step 2, and the plain blue squares, make 4 four-patch units as shown.

Make 4 each.   Make 4.

6. Attach the four-patch units to each end of the remaining units from step 4. Sew these long sections to the top and bottom of the quilt, with the gold triangles pointing away from the quilt center at each corner.

Top and Bottom Row
Make 2.

Outer Extension Rows

TO MAKE THE quilt into a rectangle, extension rows are added to the top and bottom of the quilt.

Cutting

From yellow: Cut 4 wing pairs.

From gold: Cut 8 triangle pairs.

From blue 1: Cut 4 triangle pairs.

From blue 4: Cut 4 wing pairs and 4 small plain squares.

From blue 5 and blue 6, layered wrong sides together and with blue 5 on top: Cut 4 wing pairs.

Assembly

1. Make the drunkard's squares as shown, paying careful attention to color placement.

Make 4 each.

2. Using the drunkard's squares and plain squares, piece 2 extension rows as shown. Sew the rows to the top and bottom of the quilt top so the yellow wing units point away from the quilt center at each corner.

Make 2.

Border

THE BORDER IS pieced from drunkard's squares, half–drunkard's squares, plain squares, and rectangles.

Cutting

From yellow: Cut 4 wing pairs.

From gold: Cut 4 triangle pairs.

From blue 1: Cut 4 triangle pairs.

From blue 5 and blue 6, layered wrong sides together and with blue 5 on top: Cut 4 wing pairs.

From blue 7: Cut 4 large squares, 4 small plain squares, 4 short border rectangles, and 4 long border rectangles.

Assembly

1. Make the half–drunkard's squares as shown.

Make 4 each.

2. Assemble a top and a bottom border using 2 each of the half–drunkard's squares and the long blue rectangles.

Top and Bottom Border
Make 2.

3. For the side borders, use the shorter rectangles, the small plain blue 7 squares, the remaining half–drunkard's squares, and the blue drunkard's squares. Make 2 identical borders, as shown.

Side Border
Make 2.

4. Sew the top and bottom borders to the quilt top. Press. Sew the side borders to the quilt top.

Quilt Plan

Finishing

LAYER AND BASTE your quilt top; then quilt by hand or machine. For specific details on quilting and binding, see "Techniques for Finishing," starting on page 16. You may also want to add a hanging sleeve and label to your quilt.

Dogwood Blossoms

By Mary Sue Suit, 48" x 64"

It's AMAZING HOW you can create the illusion of graceful scallops with straight-seam sewing. But that's just what happens in this quilt design, where both the white and the tan background fabrics gently undulate around the mottled pink Dogwood blocks.

You'll find the background areas are especially easy to piece, as they are made with plain squares and rectangles to fill in the large areas. The corner blocks in this quilt provide a good opportunity to use a favorite large-scale print. Use the same print for binding to tie the whole project together. For an interesting design alternative and an entirely different look, you can substitute the center block in "Stars in the Night Sky" (page 48) for the Dogwood blocks.

Quilt Sizes

Finished size of squares	Finished size of quilt
2" x 2"	24" x 32"
3" x 3"	36" x 48"
4" x 4"	48" x 64" (shown)

Materials

Yardage is based on 42"-wide fabric.

Decide the size of square you want to make; then follow the yardage requirements listed for that size.

Fabric	2" squares	3" squares	4" squares
White	½ yd.	¾ yd.	1½ yds.
Green	¼ yd.	¼ yd.	⅓ yd.
Light pink	¼ yd.	¼ yd.	½ yd.
Medium pink	¼ yd.	½ yd.	¾ yd.
Gold	¼ yd.	¼ yd.	¼ yd.
Blue	½ yd.	1 yd.	1½ yds.
Large-scale print (includes binding)	¾ yd.	¾ yd.	1 yd.
Tan	½ yd.	¾ yd.	1¼ yds.
Backing	1 yd.	1½ yds.	3⅓ yds.
Batting	28" x 36"	40" x 52"	52" x 60"

Cutting Dimensions

CUT THE FABRICS as indicated in the chart below, according to the size of drunkard's square you've chosen. The numbers of each kind of piece to cut after this first cutting are given in the directions for each section of the quilt. (Cutting the pieces when needed will help you keep track of them.)

Size of finished squares	2" x 2"	3" x 3"	4" x 4"
Size to cut strips for 45° triangles	2" x 42"	2½" x 42"	3" x 42"
Size to cut rectangles for wings	1½" x 5"	2" x 6½"	2½" x 8"
Ruler mark for cutting wings	6"	5½"	5"
Ruler mark for first trim of squares	2"	2¾"	3½"
Ruler mark for second trim of squares	2½"	3½"	4½"
Size to cut plain squares	2½" x 2½"	3½" x 3½"	4½" x 4½"
Size to cut background rectangles	2½" x 4½"	3½" x 6½"	4½" x 8½"

Dogwood Blocks

Cutting

From white: Cut 32 wing pairs.
From green: Cut 16 wing pairs.
From light pink: Cut 16 wing pairs.
From medium pink: Cut 48 triangle pairs.
From gold: Cut 16 triangle pairs.

Assembly

1. Make the drunkard's squares as shown.

Make 16 each.

2. Using 1 of each color combination, lay out and then sew a four-patch unit as shown. Repeat to make a total of 16 identical four-patch units.

Make 16.

3. Lay out 4 four-patch units as shown, rotating the units to create a Dogwood block. Sew the four-patch units together to complete the block. Repeat to make a total of 4 Dogwood blocks.

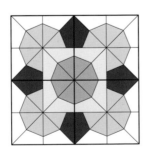

Dogwood Block
Make 4.

Background

Cutting

From blue: Cut 44 wing pairs, 4 rectangles, and 4 plain squares.
From large-scale print: Cut 12 wing pairs.
From white: Cut 20 triangle pairs.
From tan: Cut 36 triangle pairs and 16 rectangles.

Assembly

1. Make the drunkard's squares as shown. Sew 16 of them together into arch units. Set aside the remaining 4 drunkard's squares.

Make 20. Arch Unit
Make 8.

2. Make the drunkard's squares as shown.

Make 12. Make 24.

3. Sew 8 of the blue-and-tan drunkard's squares together into 4 pairs as shown.

Make 4.

4. Using 4 more of the blue-and-tan squares, sew 1 to each end of a blue-and-white arch unit, following the color placement shown. Make 2 such units; then attach them to the top of 2 of the Dogwood blocks.

Make 2.

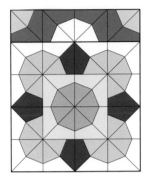

Make 2.

5. Sew 1 blue-and-tan drunkard's square to 1 end of an arch unit and a blue-and-white drunkard's square to the other end, following the color placement shown. Repeat to make a second identical unit. Then make 2 mirror-image units, as shown.

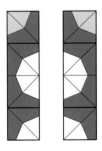

Make 2 each.

6. Using the blue-and-tan drunkard's squares, the tan rectangles, and the blue rectangles, lay out and piece 2 each of the mirror-image sections, as shown.

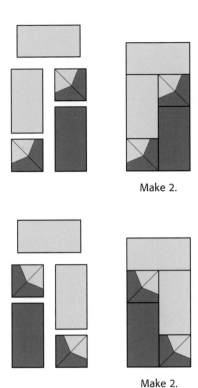

Make 2.

Make 2.

7. Using the large-scale-print drunkard's squares and tan rectangles, lay out and piece 2 of each unit shown.

Make 2 each.

8. Reserve the remaining tan rectangles and blue-and-tan drunkard's squares for the border.

9. Using the units made in steps 5–7, lay out and piece the mirror-image sections shown. Make 2 of each section.

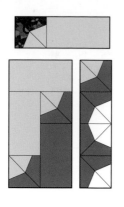 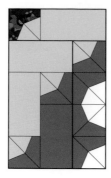

Make 2.

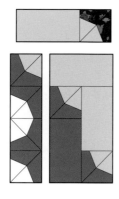 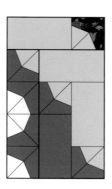

Make 2.

10. Sew 1 of each of the mirror-image sections made in step 8 to either side of a Dogwood block from step 4. The blue-and-white arch units should be facing toward the Dogwood block. Repeat to make a second identical row. These are the top and bottom rows of the quilt.

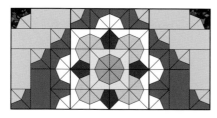

Make 2.

11. Using the remaining 2 blue-and-white arch units, sew a plain blue square to each end of the arches.

Make 2.

12. Sew each blue-and-white unit to a Dogwood block. Then stitch the two Dogwood blocks together so the blue-and-white units are on the outer edges as shown. This is the center row of the quilt.

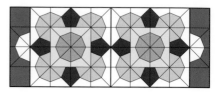

Center Row
Make 1.

13. Sew the 3 quilt rows together, referring to the quilt plan on page 59. Make sure the Dogwood blocks are all facing toward the quilt center and the background areas are on the outer edges.

Border

THE BORDER IS made with mitered corners. Refer to "Mitered Corners" on page 15 for directions, and to "Cutting Dimensions" below for the cutting measurements for your size of quilt.

Cutting Dimensions

Size of finished square	2" x 2"	3" x 3"	4" x 4"
Size to cut strips for 45° triangles	2½"	3½"	4½"
Ruler mark for long miter strip	6¼"	9¼"	12¼"
Ruler mark for short miter strip	4½"	6½"	8¼"

Cutting

From large-scale print: Cut 2 long miter corner pairs and 2 short miter corner pairs.

From tan: Cut 4 squares.

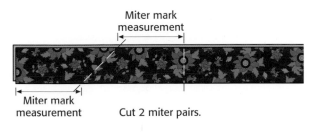

Cut 2 miter pairs.

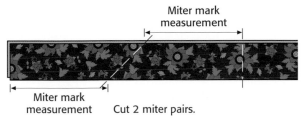

Cut 2 miter pairs.

Assembly

1. Using the remaining blue-and-tan drunkard's squares, the plain tan squares, the large-scale-print-and-tan drunkard's squares, and the short miter strips, assemble 2 borders as shown. Sew them to the top and bottom of the quilt.

Top and Bottom Border
Make 2.

2. The side borders are similar to the top and bottom borders, but they use long miter strips and tan rectangles rather than plain tan squares. Assemble 2 borders as shown; then attach them to the sides of the quilt.

Side Border
Make 2.

3. Miter the border corners, referring to "Adding Mitered Borders" on page 16.

Quilt Plan

Finishing

LAYER AND BASTE your quilt top; then quilt by hand or machine. For specific details on quilting and binding, see "Techniques for Finishing," starting on page 16. You may also want to add a hanging sleeve and label to your quilt.

Floral Bouquet

By Mary Sue Suit, 40" x 48"

Nothing brightens up a room like a spring bouquet. This quilted bouquet is made of Daffodil, Forget-Me-Not, Flower Bud, and Dogwood blocks. A few little four-patch units have also wandered into the design to create the stems for the daffodils, but other than that the design is made up of those wonderful drunkard's squares.

To make a spectacular border around the flowers, I doubled the size of drunkard's squares used for the quilt center. The quilt shown is made of 2" drunkard's squares, so the border squares are 4" each. (I've given the cutting dimensions needed for the special 6" and 8" drunkard's squares for the border in case you want to make your quilt center with 3" or 4" squares.) The larger drunkard's squares work well in the border as they provide a place to show off your hand or machine quilting.

Materials

Yardage is based on 42"-wide fabric.

Decide the size of square you want to make; then follow the yardage requirements listed for that size.

Fabric	2" squares	3" squares	4" squares
Medium blue 1	¼ yd.	¼ yd.	⅜ yd.
White	1¼ yds.	1¾ yds.	2½ yds.
Green	⅓ yd.	½ yd.	⅝ yd.
Medium blue 2	½ yd.	¾ yd.	1 yd.
Light blue	⅛ yd.	¼ yd.	¼ yd.
Medium pink	¼ yd.	¼ yd.	½ yd.
Light pink	⅛ yd.	¼ yd.	¼ yd.
Tan	2" x 20"	2½" x 22"	3" x 30"
Yellow	¼ yd.	¼ yd.	⅓ yd.
Gold	⅛ yd.	¼ yd.	¼ yd.
Light print	¾ yd.	1⅓ yds.	2⅛ yds.
Dark blue	¾ yd.	1½ yds.	2 yds.
Burgundy (includes binding)	½ yd.	1 yd.	1¼ yds.
Backing	3 yds.	4⅓ yds.	7¼ yds.
Batting	44" x 52"	64" x 76"	84" x 100"

Quilt Sizes

Finished size of squares	Finished size of quilt
2" x 2"	40" x 48" (shown)
3" x 3"	60" x 72"
4" x 4"	80" x 96"

Cutting Dimensions

CUT THE FABRICS as indicated in the chart below, according to the size of drunkard's square you've chosen. The numbers of each kind of piece to cut after this first cutting are given in the directions for each section of the quilt. (Cutting the pieces when needed will help you keep track of them.)

Size of finished squares	2" x 2"	3" x 3"	4" x 4"
Size to cut strips for 45° triangles	2" x 42"	2½" x 42"	3" x 42"
Size to cut rectangles for wings	1½" x 5"	2" x 6½"	2½" x 8"
Ruler mark for cutting wings	6"	5½"	5"
Ruler mark for first trim of squares	2"	2¾"	3½"
Ruler mark for second trim of squares	2½"	3½"	4½"
Size to cut border squares	4½" x 4½"	6½" x 6½"	8½" x 8½"
Size to cut rectangles	2½" x 4½"	3½" x 6½"	4½" x 8½"
Size to cut strips for four-patch units	1½" x 26"	2" x 36"	2½" x 42"
Size to cut plain squares	2½" x 2½"	3½" x 3½"	4½" x 4½"
Size to cut squares for half–drunkard's squares (cut in half diagonally)	3⅛" x 3⅛"	4⅛" x 4⅛"	5⅛" x 5⅛"

Forget-Me-Not Blocks

Cutting

From medium blue 1: Cut 16 wing pairs.
From white: Cut 16 triangle pairs and 16 wing pairs.
From green: Cut 16 wing pairs.
From medium blue 2: Cut 32 triangle pairs and 16 wing pairs.
From light blue: Cut 16 triangle pairs.

Assembly

1. Make the drunkard's squares as shown.

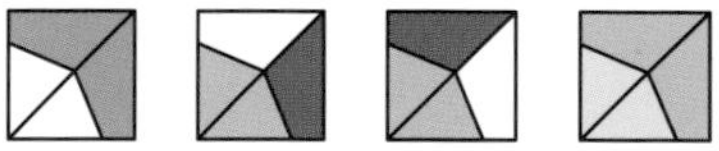

Make 16 each.

2. Using 1 drunkard's square of each color combination, lay out and piece 16 four-patch units as shown.

Make 16.

3. Arrange 4 four-patch units as shown to make a Forget-Me-Not block. Repeat to make a total of 4 blocks.

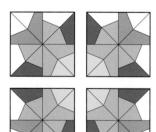 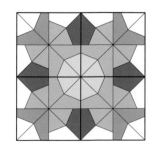

Forget-Me-Not Block
Make 4.

Dogwood Block

Cutting

From green: Cut 8 wing pairs.
From white: Cut 4 wing pairs.
From medium pink: Cut 12 triangle pairs.
From light pink: Cut 4 wing pairs.
From tan: Cut 4 triangle pairs.

Assembly

1. Make the drunkard's squares as shown.

Make 4 each.

2. Using 1 drunkard's square of each color combination, lay out and piece a four-patch unit as shown. Repeat to make 4 identical four-patch units.

Make 4.

3. Arrange the four-patch units to make 1 Dogwood block as shown.

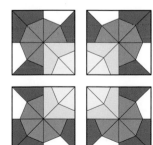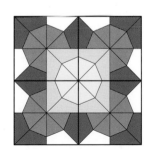

Dogwood Block
Make 1.

Flower Bud Blocks

Each Flower Bud block is made of 2 bud units and 2 plain squares. The size to cut the squares depends on which size of drunkard's squares you are making. Refer to "Cutting Dimensions" on page 62 for the appropriate sizes to cut.

Cutting

From white: Cut 4 plain squares, 4 triangle pairs, and 8 wing pairs.
From light pink: Cut 4 wing pairs.
From green: Cut 4 wing pairs.
From medium pink: Cut 12 triangle pairs.

Assembly

1. Make the drunkard's squares as shown.

Make 4 each.   Make 8.

2. Using 2 pink-and-white drunkard's squares and 1 of each of the other 2 color combinations, lay out and piece 4 four-patch units as shown.

Flower Bud Unit
Make 4.

3. Add the plain white squares to the four-patch units as shown, to complete the Flower Bud blocks. Note that you are piecing mirror-image blocks. Make 2 of each.

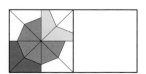

Flower Bud Blocks
Make 2 each.

Daffodil Blocks

SEE "CUTTING DIMENSIONS" on page 62 for measurements needed to cut strips for the four-patch units and squares for the half–drunkard's squares.

Cutting

From white: Cut 1 strip for four-patch units, 8 rectangles, 24 wing pairs, and 12 triangle pairs.

From green: Cut 1 strip for four-patch units and 8 wing pairs.

From yellow: Cut 4 half–drunkard's squares, 8 triangle pairs, 4 wing pairs, and 4 small plain squares.

From gold: Cut 8 triangle pairs and 8 half–drunkard's squares.

Assembly

1. Make the drunkard's squares as shown.

Make 4.   Make 8 each.

2. Make the half–drunkard's squares as shown.

Make 8 each.

3. Sew the green strip to the white strip, right sides together. Press the seam allowance toward the green fabric. Cut the strip set into segments that are the same width as the strips you started with (1½", 2", or 2½"). Cut 16 segments.

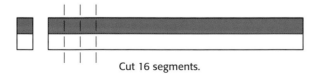

Cut 16 segments.

4. Sew the segments together in pairs to form 8 four-patch units as shown.

Make 8.

5. Using the yellow-and-white drunkard's squares and the small yellow plain squares, assemble 4 four-patch units as shown.

Make 4.

6. Using the green-and-white four-patch units, the gold-and-white drunkard's squares, and the half–drunkard's squares, assemble 4 each of the units shown.

Make 4 each.

7. Add the units made in step 6 to the daffodil units made in step 5.

 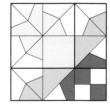

Make 4.

8. Using the gold-and-white half–drunkard's squares, the white rectangles, and the remaining green-and-white four-patch units, make 4 each of the units shown below.

Make 4 each.

9. Add the units made in step 8 to the daffodil units made in step 7 to complete 4 Daffodil blocks.

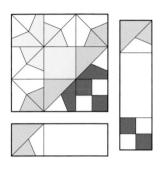

Daffodil Block
Make 4.

Quilt Assembly

1. Make 2 rows using 2 Daffodil blocks, 2 Flower Bud blocks, and 1 Forget-Me-Not block, orienting the blocks as shown below. These are the right and left vertical rows.

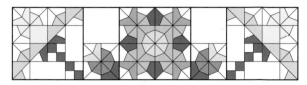

Make 2.

2. For the center vertical row, sew a Forget-Me-Not block on either side of the Dogwood block. Set the rows aside; don't sew them together yet.

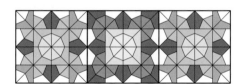

Make 1.

Borders

THE BORDERS ARE made of drunkard's squares that are twice the size of the squares used in the center of the quilt. The cutting dimensions for these larger squares are provided below.

Cutting Dimensions

Size of finished squares	2" x 2"	3" x 3"	4" x 4"
Size of finished border squares	4" x 4"	6" x 6"	8" x 8"
Size to cut strips for 45° triangles	3" x 42"	4" x 42"	5" x 42"
Size to cut rectangles for wings	2½" x 8"	3½" x 13"	4½" x 13½"
Ruler mark for cutting wings	5"	4"	3¼"
Ruler mark for first trim of squares	3"	5"	6¼"
Ruler mark for second trim of squares	4½"	6½"	8½"
Size to cut plain border squares	4½" x 4½"	6½" x 6½"	8½" x 8½"
Size to cut border rectangles	4½" x 8½"	6½" x 12½"	8½" x 16½"

Cutting

From white: Cut 28 wing pairs.

From light print: Cut 28 triangle pairs and 32 triangle pairs.

From dark blue: Cut 8 plain border squares, 2 border rectangles, 4 triangle pairs, and 32 wing pairs.

From burgundy: Cut 4 wing pairs.

Assembly

1. Make the drunkard's squares for the inner border as shown. Sew them together in pairs.

  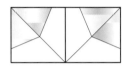

Make 12.

  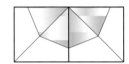

Make 2.

2. Sew the 2 pairs where the triangles are joined to either end of the center row.

3. Sew the 3 flower rows together, with the daffodil rows on the outside edges, pointing toward the outer corners of the quilt top.

4. Make the drunkard's squares for the outer border as shown.

Make 4.   Make 32.

5. Sew the dark-blue-and-light-print drunkard's squares together in pairs, as shown.

Make 12.   Make 2.

6. Using the drunkard's squares, the plain squares, rectangles, and the units pieced in step 5, make the border units as shown.

Make 2.   Make 4.

Make 12.

7. Make 2 side borders by sewing together the dark blue, light print, and white units. Each side border contains 4 of these units. Stitch the side borders to the quilt top.

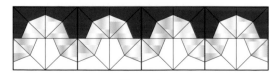

Side Border
Make 2.

8. Make the top and bottom borders by sewing the remaining units together. Sew the top and bottom borders to the quilt top, making sure the burgundy wings in each corner are pointing outward.

Top and Bottom Border
Make 2.

Finishing

LAYER AND BASTE your quilt top; then quilt by hand or machine. For specific details on quilting and binding, see "Techniques for Finishing," starting on page 16. You may also want to add a hanging sleeve and label to your quilt.

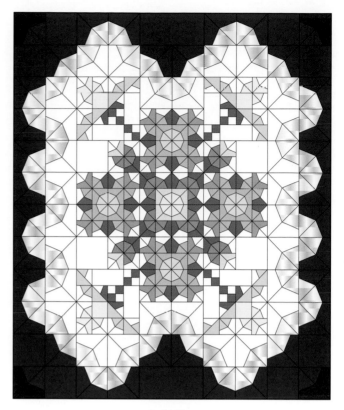

Quilt Plan

Rosa Lee

BY MARY SUE SUIT, 32" x 44"

Quilt Sizes

Finished size of squares	Finished size of quilt
2" x 2"	32" x 44" (shown)
3" x 3"	48" x 66"
4" x 4"	64" x 88"

Materials

Yardage is based on 42"-wide fabric.

Decide the size of square you want to make; then follow the yardage requirements listed for that size.

Fabric	2" squares	3" squares	4" squares
White	1½ yds.	2½ yds.	2¾ yds.
Burgundy	⅓ yd.	½ yd.	¾ yd.
Light pink	⅓ yd.	½ yd.	¾ yd.
Medium pink	¼ yd.	¼ yd.	⅜ yd.
Medium-dark pink	¼ yd.	¼ yd.	⅜ yd.
Green	½ yd.	¾ yd.	1 yd.
Dark green	¼ yd.	¼ yd.	⅜ yd.
Floral print	¾ yd.	1¼ yds.	1½ yds.
Backing	1⅜ yds.	3 yds.	5¼ yds.
Binding	½ yd.	¾ yd.	1 yd.
Batting	36" x 48"	52" x 70"	68" x 92"

DAINTY PINK ROSEBUDS are scattered all along the garden path in this quilt design. Once you make the Rosebud blocks, it's an easy stroll. To give the rosebuds depth, I used four values in the pink family: light, medium, medium-dark, and dark. Feel free to choose any color family for your rosebuds that pleases you. Reds, yellows, apricots, even lavenders make a nice arrangement as long as you work in the four values. You can further customize your design by changing the number of roses.

As in "Floral Bouquet" (page 60), the drunkard's squares in this quilt's border are twice the size of those in the quilt's center. It's an effective way to emphasize the border without doing an excessive amount of piecing. Plus, whether you like to quilt by hand or by machine, the large open areas give you a place to show off your quilting prowess.

Cutting Dimensions

CUT THE FABRICS as indicated in the chart below, according to the size of drunkard's square you've chosen. The numbers of each kind of piece to cut after this first cutting are given in the directions for each section of the quilt. (Cutting the pieces when needed will help you keep track of them.)

Size of finished squares	2" x 2"	3" x 3"	4" x 4"
Size to cut strips for 45° triangles	2" x 42"	2½" x 42"	3" x 42"
Size to cut rectangles for wings	1½" x 5"	2" x 6½"	2½" x 8"
Ruler mark for cutting wings	6"	5½"	5"
Ruler mark for first trim of squares	2"	2¾"	3½"
Ruler mark for second trim of squares	2½"	3½"	4½"

Rosebud Blocks

Cutting

From white: Cut 24 wing pairs and 24 triangle pairs.
From burgundy: Cut 48 wing pairs.
From light pink: Cut 24 wing pairs.
From medium pink: Cut 36 triangle pairs.
From medium-dark pink: Cut 36 triangle pairs.

Fabric Color Key

Light pink		White	
Medium pink		Green	
Medium-dark pink		Dark green	
Burgundy		Floral print	

Assembly

1. Make the drunkard's squares as shown, paying careful attention to color placement.

Make 12 each.

2. Using 1 drunkard's square of each color combination, piece a Rosebud block as shown. Repeat to make 12 identical blocks.

Rosebud Block
Make 12.

3. Make the drunkard's squares as shown. Note that these squares are the mirror images of the ones made in step 1.

Make 12 each.

4. Using 1 drunkard's square of each color combination, piece a Rosebud block as shown. Repeat to make 12 identical blocks. Note that these blocks are the mirror image of the blocks made in step 2.

Rosebud Block
Make 12.

Cross Blocks

Cutting

From light pink: Cut 24 wing pairs.
From white: Cut 24 triangle pairs.

Assembly

1. Make the drunkard's squares as shown.

Make 24.

2. Lay out and piece 6 Cross blocks, with the light-pink triangles pointing toward the centers of the blocks.

Cross Block
Make 6.

Pathway Blocks

Cutting

From white: Cut 96 wing pairs.
From green: Cut 72 triangle pairs.
From dark green: Cut 24 triangle pairs.

Assembly

1. Make the drunkard's squares as shown.

Make 48.   Make 24 each.

2. Lay out and piece 24 Pathway blocks as shown, paying careful attention to color placement so the dark green triangles are side by side in the top row.

Pathway Block
Make 24.

Row Assembly

THE QUILT CENTER is made up of 2 different rows, A and B. Pay careful attention to color placement so you don't mix up the mirror-image Rosebud blocks.

1. Make 6 of row A and 3 of row B, as shown.

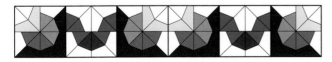

Row A
Make 6.

Row B
Make 3.

2. Sew the rows together, following the sequence A-B-A-A-B-A-A-B-A. Note that not all of the A rows face in the same direction. Some have the center arch facing upward; others have the arch facing downward, so pay careful attention to the orientation of each row as you sew them together.

Border

THE BORDER IS made of drunkard's squares twice the size of the blocks used in the quilt center. The cutting dimensions for these larger blocks are provided below.

Cutting Dimensions

Size of finished squares	2" x 2"	3" x 3"	4" x 4"
Size of blocks	4" x 4"	6" x 6"	8" x 8"
Size to cut strips for 45° triangles	3" x 42"	4" x 42"	5" x 42"
Size to cut rectangles for wings	2½" x 8"	3½" x 13"	4½" x 13½"
Ruler mark for cutting wings	5"	4"	3¼"
Ruler mark for first trim of squares	3"	5"	6¼"
Ruler mark for second trim of squares	4½"	6½"	8½"
Size to cut plain border squares	4½" x 4½"	6½" x 6½"	8½" x 8½"
Size to cut border rectangles	4½" x 8½"	6½" x 12½"	8½" x 16½"

Cutting

From floral print: Cut 24 wing pairs, 4 plain border squares, and 4 border rectangles.

From white: Cut 24 triangle pairs.

Assembly

1. Make the drunkard's squares as shown. Sew them together in pairs to make arch units.

Make 24.

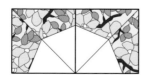

Arch Unit
Make 12.

2. Using the border rectangles, the plain border squares, and the arch units, piece 2 side borders and the top and bottom borders as shown.

Side Border
Make 2.

Top and Bottom Border
Make 2.

3. Sew the side borders to the quilt; then, referring to the quilt plans, attach the top and bottom borders.

Quilt Plan

Finishing

LAYER AND BASTE your quilt top; then quilt by hand or machine. For specific details on quilting and binding, see "Techniques for Finishing," starting on page 16. You may also want to add a hanging sleeve and label to your quilt.

A Leap of Faith

BY JUDY WOODWORTH, 82" x 90"

THIS QUILT IS a wonderful example of the rewards of having faith. I asked my friend Judy to try out the directions for constructing drunkard's squares and perhaps make a quilt to be shared with you. Judy showed faith in my directions and jumped right in—and I had faith in her talents as a quiltmaker. It came as no surprise to me that her quilt is simply wonderful. "A Leap of Faith" shows what can be done with one little square, an interesting piece of fabric, and a little imagination.

Xanablue

By Mary Sue Suit, 20" x 20"

This little gem is made with four blocks that are as close to traditional Drunkard's Path blocks as I get. I arranged them in a Wonder of the World setting that has a clockwise spinning motion, but that's where the similarity ends.

Upon close examination, you'll see that my blocks spin in both directions. I set them this way to avoid having bias triangle edges on the outside edges of the blocks. I used twelve different blue fabrics, plus white and a mottled fabric for the background. All these shades of blue add to the excitement and increase the sense of movement within the blocks.

To make cutting and piecing a cinch, number your blues from one to twelve so you won't go wrong. Of course, if you don't enjoy being that regimented, simply use your blue fabrics randomly—this block is a perfect candidate for an all-out scrap party.

Quilt Sizes

Finished size of squares	Finished size of quilt
2" x 2"	20" x 20" (shown)
3" x 3"	30" x 30"
4" x 4"	40" x 40"

Materials

Yardage is based on 42"-wide fabric.

Decide the size of square you want to make; then follow the yardage requirements listed for that size.

Fabric	2" squares	3" squares	4" squares
12 different blues	2" x 42" strip of *each*	2½" x 42" strip of *each*	⅛ yd. fabrics 1–4 and 7–10; ¼ yd. fabrics 5, 6, 11, and 12
Mottled background	½ yd.	½ yd.	⅔ yd.
White	½ yd.	¾ yd.	1 yd.
Backing	¾ yd.	1 yd.	1⅜ yds.
Binding	½ yd.	½ yd.	1 yd.
Batting	24" x 24"	34" x 34"	44" x 44"

Cutting Dimensions

Cut the fabrics as indicated in the chart below, according to the size of drunkard's square you've chosen. The numbers of each kind of piece to cut after this first cutting are given in the directions for each section of the quilt. (Cutting the pieces when needed will help you keep track of them.)

Size of finished squares	2" x 2"	3" x 3"	4" x 4"
Size to cut strips for 45° triangles	2" x 42"	2½" x 42"	3" x 42"
Size to cut rectangles for wings	1½" x 5"	2" x 6½"	2½" x 8"
Ruler mark for cutting wings	6"	5½"	5"
Ruler mark for first trim of squares	2"	2¾"	3½"
Ruler mark for second trim of squares	2½"	3½"	4½"
Size to cut squares for half–drunkard's squares (cut in half diagonally)	3⅛" x 3⅛"	4⅛" x 4⅛"	5⅛" x 5⅛"
Size to cut border rectangles	2½" x 8½"	3½" x 12½"	4½" x 16½"

Xanablue Blocks

Cutting

From *each* of 12 different blues: Cut 2 triangle pairs. (Note: Cut these before cutting any of the blue wing pairs listed below.)

From mottled background: Cut 32 wing pairs.

From white: Cut 16 wing pairs and 16 triangle pairs.

From blue 5 and blue 6, layered wrong sides together and with blue 6 on top: Cut 8 wing pairs.

From blue 10 and blue 11, layered wrong sides together and with blue 11 on top: Cut 8 wing pairs.

Fabric Color Key

▩ Blue 1	▩ Blue 4	▩ Blue 7	▩ Blue 10
▩ Blue 2	▩ Blue 5	▩ Blue 8	▩ Blue 11
▩ Blue 3	▩ Blue 6	▩ Blue 9	▩ Blue 12

Assembly

1. Make the drunkard's squares as shown. These combinations use triangles cut from blues 1–6 and wings cut from blue 7 and blue 8. Unless you're making a scrappy version, pay careful attention to the color placement.

Make 4 each.

2. Sew 1 drunkard's square of each of the color combinations together to make a four-patch unit as shown. Repeat to make 3 more identical units.

Make 4.

3. Make the drunkard's squares as shown, paying close attention to color placement.

Make 4 each.

4. Sew 1 drunkard's square of each of the color combinations together to make a four-patch unit as shown. Repeat to make 3 more identical units.

Make 4.

5. Using 2 of the four-patch units made in step 2, and 2 of the units made in step 4, piece a Xanablue block that rotates clockwise. Repeat.

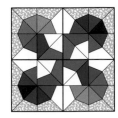

Clockwise Xanablue Block
Make 2.

6. Using the remaining triangles and wings, make the drunkard's squares as shown.

Make 4 each.

7. Using 1 drunkard's square of each color combination, make 4 four-patch units as shown.

Make 4.

8. Make the drunkard's squares as shown.

Make 4 each.

9. Using 1 drunkard's square of each color combination, make 4 four-patch units as shown.

 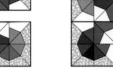

Make 4.

10. Using 2 of the four-patch units made in step 7, and 2 of the units made in step 8, make 2 Xanablue blocks that rotate counterclockwise. Repeat.

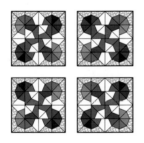

Counterclockwise
Xanablue Block
Make 2.

11. Alternating the 2 types of blocks, sew them together to complete the center of the quilt top.

Border

Cutting

From white: Cut 4 border rectangles and 12 triangle pairs.
From mottled background: Cut 8 large squares.
From blue 12: Cut 12 wing pairs.

Assembly

1. Make the drunkard's squares and half–drunkard's squares as shown.

Make 4.   Make 8 each.

2. Sew the mirror-image half–drunkard's squares together into pairs so the blue triangles are touching, as shown.

Make 8.

3. For the side borders, sew a pair of half–drunkard's squares to either end of 2 of the white border rectangles. Repeat for the top and bottom borders. Then sew a drunkard's square to each end of the top and bottom borders.

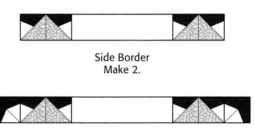

Side Border
Make 2.

Top and Bottom Border
Make 2.

4. Sew the side borders to the quilt top, then the top and bottom borders.

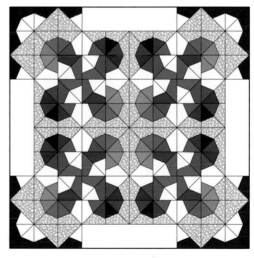

Quilt Plan

Finishing

LAYER AND BASTE your quilt top; then quilt by hand or machine. For specific details on quilting and binding, see "Techniques for Finishing," starting on page 16. You may also want to add a hanging sleeve and label to your quilt.

Magic Carpet

BY MARY SUE SUIT, 66" x 72"

CRISSCROSSING PATHS IN rich hues form a medallion design reminiscent of an Oriental carpet. While the look is magical, this project isn't for the faint of heart. It can be a real puzzler because there are so many mirror-image blocks in the quilt, but the puzzle is all part of the fun. The drunkard's squares are made just as for all the other projects; you simply need to pay careful attention to the rotation. Just a quarter turn in the wrong direction, and you could be off on a totally different path!

Choose two color families for this quilt (I used rust and teal); then select a dark and medium fabric from each color. I let the colors in my print fabric lead the way. If you're ready for a challenge, I encourage you to try this pattern. Remember, it's the path least taken that can lead to the greatest rewards.

Materials

Yardage is based on 42"-wide fabric.

Decide the size of square you want to make; then follow the yardage requirements listed for that size.

Fabric	2" squares	3" squares	4" squares
Medium background	1¼ yds.	2 yds.	2¾ yds.
Dark blue print	1 yd.	1¼ yds.	1⅝ yds.
Dark teal (includes binding)	1⅓ yds.	1¾ yds.	2⅓ yds.
Medium teal	¼ yd.	½ yd.	⅝ yd.
Dark rust	¾ yd.	1¼ yds.	1⅝ yds.
Medium rust	⅔ yd.	1 yd.	1⅝ yds.
Brown	¾ yd.	1⅛ yds.	1¾ yds.
Light background	1¼ yds.	2¼ yds.	3¼ yds.
Backing	2¾ yds.	4 yds.	7¾ yds.
Batting	48" x 52"	70" x 76"	92" x 100"

Quilt Sizes

Finished size of squares	Finished size of quilt
2" x 2"	44" x 48"
3" x 3"	66" x 72" (shown)
4" x 4"	88" x 96"

Cutting Dimensions

CUT THE FABRICS as indicated in the chart below, according to the size of drunkard's square you've chosen. The numbers of each kind of piece to cut after this first cutting are given in the directions for each section of the quilt. (Cutting the pieces when needed will help you keep track of them.)

Size of finished squares	2" x 2"	3" x 3"	4" x 4"
Size to cut strips for 45° triangles	2" x 42"	2½" x 42"	3" x 42"
Size to cut rectangles for wings	1½" x 5"	2" x 6½"	2½" x 8"
Ruler mark for cutting wings	6"	5½"	5"
Ruler mark for first trim of squares	2"	2¾"	3½"
Ruler mark for second trim of squares	2½"	3½"	4½"
Size to cut small rectangles	2½" x 4½"	3½" x 6½"	4½" x 8½"
Size to cut small squares	2½" x 2½"	3½" x 3½"	4½" x 4½"
Size to cut large squares	4½" x 4½"	6½" x 6½"	8½" x 8½"
Size to cut large rectangles	2½" x 6½"	3½" x 9½"	4½" x 12½"

Quilt Center

Cutting

From medium background: Cut 32 triangle pairs and 32 wing pairs.
From dark blue print: Cut 32 triangle pairs.
From dark teal: Cut 8 wing pairs.
From medium teal: Cut 8 wing pairs.
From dark rust: Cut 8 wing pairs.
From medium rust: Cut 8 wing pairs.

Fabric Color Key

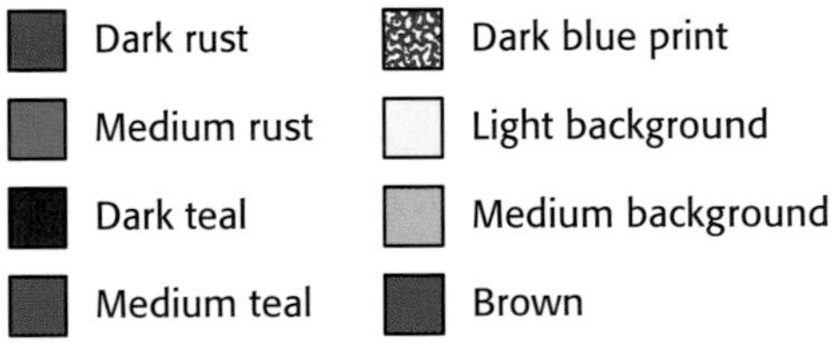

Dark rust
Medium rust
Dark teal
Medium teal
Dark blue print
Light background
Medium background
Brown

Assembly

1. Make the drunkard's squares as shown.

Make 8 each.　　　　Make 32.

2. Four types of four-patch units, 2 of each color family, are used to make blocks A and B. Make 4 of the block A four-patch units using teal fabrics and 4 using rust fabrics. Also make 4 of the block B four-patch units using teal fabrics and 4 using rust fabrics. Notice that the dark blue triangles always point toward the center of the blocks. The other drunkard's squares are always placed so they look like a capital L. But the placement changes for the other colors. In the block A four-patch units, the dark teal and dark rust are in the upper left corners. In the block B four-patch units, the light teal and light rust are in the upper left corners.

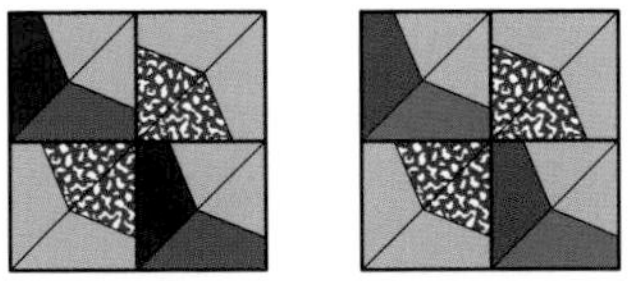

Block A Four-Patch Units
Make 4 each.

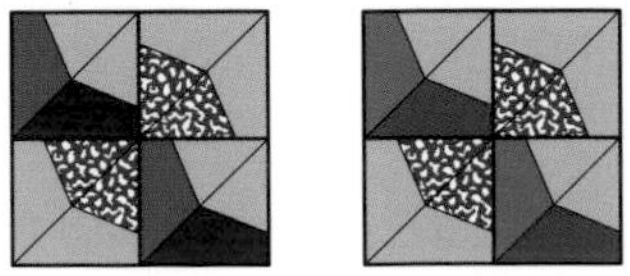

Block B Four-Patch Units
Make 4 each.

3. Using the teal block A and rust block A four-patch units, make 2 of block A.

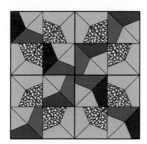

Block A
Make 2.

4. Using the teal block B and rust block B four-patch units, make 2 of block B.

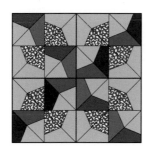

Block B
Make 2.

5. Alternating the blocks, sew them together into a large four-patch unit for the center of the quilt.

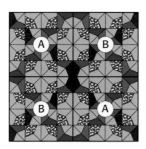

Quilt Center

First Round

THE QUILT CENTER is surrounded by several rounds. The first round is similar to a border. It uses plain squares and rectangles. The sizes to cut the pieces are provided in "Cutting Dimensions" on page 80.

Cutting

From medium background: Cut 24 wing pairs, 16 triangle pairs, 4 small rectangles, 4 small squares, and 4 large squares.
From dark rust: Cut 8 triangle pairs and 2 wing pairs.
From dark teal: Cut 12 triangle pairs.
From medium rust: Cut 2 wing pairs.
From brown: Cut 12 wing pairs.

Assembly

1. Make the drunkard's squares as shown, paying careful attention to color placement.

Make 8.   Make 12 each.   Make 2 each.

2. Sew the drunkard's squares together in pairs as shown.

Make 4.   Make 4.   Make 2.

3. For the side rounds, sew a small rectangle to both sides of a dark rust arch pair; then sew a single dark teal drunkard's square to both ends of the row. Sew these rows to the sides of the quilt with the rust and teal fabrics joining the quilt center.

Make 2.

4. With the remaining drunkard's squares and the small squares, make 2 each of the four-patch units shown.

Make 2 each.

5. To make the top and bottom rows, sew the four-patch units from step 4 to the large squares as

shown. Sew the rows to the top and bottom of the quilt center with the teal fabric joining the quilt.

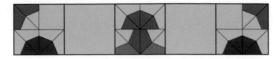

Make 2.

Second Round

Cutting

From brown: Cut 32 wing pairs, 8 triangle pairs, 4 small rectangles, and 4 large rectangles.

From dark teal: Cut 24 triangle pairs.

From dark rust: Cut 8 wing pairs.

From medium rust: Cut 8 wing pairs.

From light background: Cut 8 triangle pairs and 4 small squares.

Assembly

1. Make the drunkard's squares as shown, paying careful attention to color placement.

Make 24.   Make 2 each.

2. Sew the brown-and-teal drunkard's squares into arch units. Sew the medium-background-and-brown drunkard's squares remaining from step 1 of "First Round" into arch units.

Make 12.   Make 4.

3. Using the arch units, the small rectangles, and the drunkard's squares with the light background triangles, make 2 side strips. Sew them to the sides of the quilt so the teal fabric is not joining the quilt center.

Side Strip
Make 2.

4. Make top and bottom strips using the large rectangles, the dark teal arch units, the drunkard's squares with brown triangles, and the light background squares. Sew them to the top and bottom of the quilt center so the teal fabric is not joining the quilt center. Reserve the remaining dark teal arch units for the border.

Top and Bottom Strip
Make 2.

Third Round

Cutting

From light background: Cut 64 triangle pairs and 64 wing pairs.

From dark blue print: Cut 64 triangle pairs.

From dark teal: Cut 16 wing pairs.

From medium teal: Cut 16 wing pairs.

From dark rust: Cut 16 wing pairs.

From medium rust: Cut 16 wing pairs.

Assembly

1. Make the drunkard's squares as shown, paying careful attention to color placement.

Make 16 each.   Make 64.

2. Assemble the drunkard's squares into four-patch units. These units are identical to the units for blocks A and B made earlier, with one exception—they use light background instead of medium background fabric. Make 8 of each color combination.

Block C Four-Patch Units
Make 8 each.

Block D Four-Patch Units
Make 8 each.

3. Using the block C four-patch units, make 4 of block C.

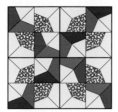

Block C
Make 4.

4. Using the block D four-patch units, make 4 of block D.

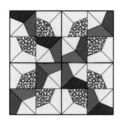

Block D
Make 4.

5. Sew blocks C and D together in pairs, with block D on the left and block C on the right. Set them aside.

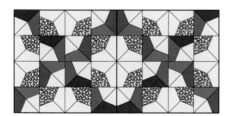

Make 4.

Medallion Blocks

Cutting

From dark rust: Cut 20 wing pairs and 16 triangle pairs.

From medium rust: Cut 20 wing pairs and 16 triangle pairs.

From light background: Cut 40 triangle pairs, 4 wing pairs, and 4 small triangles.

From dark teal: Cut 4 triangle pairs.

From dark blue print: Cut 16 wing pairs.

Assembly

1. Make the drunkard's squares as shown, paying careful attention to color placement. Reserve extra rust triangles for the Half Medallion blocks.

Make 20 each.　　Make 4.　　Make 16.

2. Make 4 of each of the four-patch units as shown, paying careful attention to the color placement. Notice that all the blocks use the same color placement except for the upper left corner.

Make 4 each.

3. Using the four-patch units, lay out and piece 4 Medallion blocks as shown. Each one is slightly different from the others, so pay careful attention to color placement.

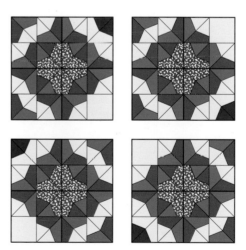

Make 1 each.

4. Add the complete Medallion blocks to 2 of the units made in step 5 of "Third Round." Do not attach these to the quilt yet.

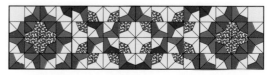

Make 2.

Half Medallion Blocks

Cutting

From dark rust: Cut 16 wing pairs.

From medium rust: Cut 16 wing pairs.

From light background: Cut 32 triangle pairs and
4 wing pairs.

From dark teal: Cut 4 triangle pairs.

From dark blue print: Cut 16 wing pairs.

Assembly

1. Make the drunkard's squares as shown, using the
leftover rust triangles from the Medallion blocks.

Make 16 each.   Make 16.   Make 4.

2. Lay out and piece 4 of each type of four-patch
unit. Sew them together in pairs to make Half
Medallion blocks. Reserve the remaining drunkard's squares for the quilt corners.

Make 4 each.

Make 2 each.

3. Sew a Half Medallion block to each end of the
remaining 2 units made in step 5 of "Third
Round." Sew these units to the top and bottom
of the quilt top.

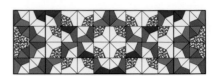

Top and Bottom Row
Make 2.

Corners

THE CORNERS ARE made of drunkard's squares,
plain squares, and miter strips. The cutting and marking dimensions for the squares and miter strips are
provided below.

Cutting Dimensions

Size of finished squares	2" x 2"	3" x 3"	4" x 4"
Size to cut plain squares	2½" x 2½"	3½" x 3½"	4½" x 4½"
Size to cut miter strips	2½" x 42"	3½" x 42"	4½" x 42"
Ruler mark for miter cut	2¼"	3¼"	4¼"

Cutting

From medium background: Cut miter strips (one
2½", four 3½", or four 4½" strips, depending
on the size of blocks you are making) and 12
wing pairs.

From light background: Cut 12 triangle pairs and
4 plain squares.

Assembly

1. Make the drunkard's squares as shown.

Make 12.

2. Using the leftover drunkard's squares from the Half Medallion blocks and the light-and-medium-background drunkard's squares pieced in step 1, assemble 2 of each of the 2 units shown below.

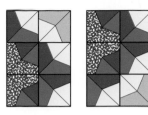

Make 2 each.

3. Cut 4 miter corner pairs, using sizes and marks given in "Cutting Dimensions" on page 84.

Miter mark measurement

Fold

Miter mark measurement

Cut 4 miter corner pairs.

4. Sew 4 light-and-medium-background drunkard's squares to a plain light-background square. Sew the miter corner pairs to the remaining 4 drunkard's squares as shown.

Make 2 each.   Make 4.

5. Sew the units from step 4 together to make 4 corner sections. Sew the corner sections to the units made in step 2, as shown.

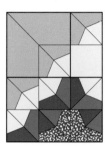 

Make 2 each.

6. Sew the corner sections to the units made in step 4 of "Medallion Blocks," then attach them to the sides of the quilt.

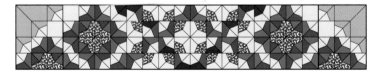

Make 2.

Border

THE BORDER IS made of drunkard's squares, border rectangles, and miter stips. The cutting dimensions for the border rectangles and the miter strips are provided below.

Border Cutting

Size of finished squares	2" x 2"	3" x 3"	4" x 4"
Size to cut rectangles	2½" x 4½"	3½" x 6½"	4½" x 8½"
Size to cut miter strips	2½" x 42"	3½" x 42"	4½" x 42"
Ruler mark for short miter cuts	10¼"	15¼"	20¼"
Ruler mark for long miter cuts	14¼"	21¼"	28¼"

Additional Cutting

From brown: Cut 4 strips for miter pieces,
8 rectangles, and 8 wing pairs.

From dark rust: Cut 8 triangle pairs.

Assembly

1. Make the drunkard's squares as shown. Sew
them together to make arch pairs.

Make 8.   Make 4.

2. Using the dark rust arch pairs, the border rectangles, and the dark teal arch pairs reserved
from "Second Round" on page 82, make 4 partial borders, as shown.

Partial Border
Make 4.

3. Using the brown miter strips, cut 2 short miter
pairs and sew them to the ends of 2 partial borders for the top and bottom of the quilt. Cut 2
long miter pairs and sew them to the remaining
2 partial borders for the sides of the quilt. Add
the borders in a clockwise fashion, referring to
"Adding Mitered Borders" on page 16 for details.

Quilt Plan

Finishing

LAYER AND BASTE your quilt top; then quilt by hand
or machine. For specific details on quilting and binding, see "Techniques for Finishing," starting on page
16. You may also want to add a hanging sleeve and
label to your quilt.

Mallo

BY BECKY UMENTHUM, 24" x 28"

"MALLO" IS BECKY'S creative interpretation of the center of "Magic Carpet." She used 2" squares and a variation in the background value placement, choosing a light fabric for the center of the quilt and a slightly darker one to go around the outside.

Pathway to the Stars

By Mary Sue Suit, 80" x 96". Machine quilted by Judy Woodworth.

SPRING GREENS, LAVENDERS, and peachy golds combine to make a lovely path. I based my color scheme on the cheery pansy print I wanted to use. You can do the same—pick a floral or other print that has a variety of colors in it, and use it as your color guide.

The half–drunkard's squares make it easy to create stars surrounded by white halos. You'll also find it easy to assemble this quilt, even though it looks a little tricky. While the pathways form a center diamond design, the quilt is pieced in quarters and in straight-set rows. What could be easier?

Materials

Yardage is based on 42"-wide fabric.

Decide the size of square you want to make; then follow the yardage requirements listed for that size.

Fabric	2" squares	3" squares	4" squares
Light lavender	1 yd.	1¼ yds.	1¾ yds.
Dark green	1 yd.	1¼ yds.	1¾ yds.
White	¾ yd.	1 yd.	1¼ yds.
Dark print	1 yd.	1¼ yds.	1¾ yds.
Light gold	½ yd.	⅔ yd.	1 yd.
Medium lavender	¾ yd.	1 yd.	1½ yds.
Medium gold	⅓ yd.	⅓ yd.	½ yd.
Light green	½ yd.	¾ yd.	1 yd.
Dark lavender	¼ yd.	½ yd.	½ yd.
Medium green	½ yd.	½ yd.	¾ yd.
Backing	2½ yds.	3⅝ yds.	7⅛ yds.
Binding	½ yd.	¾ yd.	1 yd.
Batting	44" x 52"	64" x 76"	84" x 100"

Quilt Sizes

Finished size of squares	Finished size of quilt
2" x 2"	40" x 48"
3" x 3"	60" x 72"
4" x 4"	80" x 96" (shown)

Cutting Dimensions

Cut the fabrics as indicated in the chart below, according to the size of drunkard's square you've chosen. The numbers of each kind of piece to cut after this first cutting are given in the directions for each section of the quilt. (Cutting the pieces when needed will help you keep track of them.)

Size of finished squares	2" x 2"	3" x 3"	4" x 4"
Size to cut strips for 45° triangles	2" x 42"	2½" x 42"	3" x 42"
Size to cut rectangles for wings	1½" x 5"	2" x 6½"	2½" x 8"
Ruler mark for cutting wings	6"	5½"	5"
Ruler mark for first trim of squares	2"	2¾"	3½"
Ruler mark for second trim of squares	2½"	3½"	4½"
Size to cut small squares	2½" x 2½"	3½" x 3½"	4½" x 4½"
Size to cut large squares	4½" x 4½"	6½" x 6½"	8½" x 8½"
Size to cut strips for borders	2½" x 42"	3½" x 42"	4½" x 42"
Ruler mark for corner miters	10¼"	15¼"	20¼"
Size to cut inner border rectangles	2½" x 12½"	3½" x 18½"	4½" x 24½"
Size to cut outer border rectangles	2½" x 8½"	3½" x 12½"	4½" x 16½"

Quilt Construction

This quilt is easiest to make by piecing it in 4 quarters rather than sewing together individual blocks and rows. Below are instructions for making the various four-patch units you'll need to assemble the quilt in this manner, rather than individual block instructions.

Center Star Four-Patch Units

Cutting

From light lavender: Cut 16 wing pairs and 16 small squares.
From dark green: Cut 16 wing pairs.
From white: Cut 16 triangle pairs.
From dark print: Cut 32 triangle pairs.
From light gold: Cut 16 wing pairs.

Assembly

1. Make the drunkard's squares as shown, paying careful attention to color placement.

Make 16 each.

2. Using 1 of each color combination of drunkard's squares and the light lavender small squares, lay out and piece a four-patch unit as shown. Repeat to make a total of 16 four-patch units.

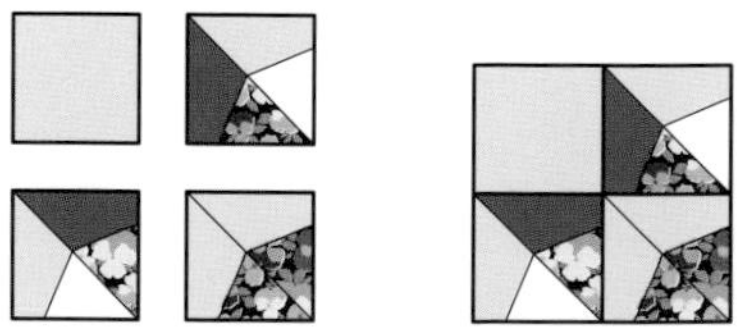

Make 16.

Light Lavender Path Units

Cutting

From light lavender: Cut 48 wing pairs.
From white: Cut 16 triangle pairs.
From dark green: Cut 32 triangle pairs.
From light gold: Cut 16 wing pairs.
From dark print: Cut 16 wing pairs.

Assembly

1. Make the drunkard's squares as shown.

Make 16 each.   Make 32.

2. Using 2 drunkard's squares with dark green triangles and 1 each with white and dark print triangles, lay out and piece a four-patch unit as shown. Repeat to make a total of 16 four-patch units.

Make 16.

Medium Lavender Path Units

Cutting

From light gold: Cut 8 wing pairs.
From dark print: Cut 8 triangle pairs.
From medium lavender: Cut 24 wing pairs.
From white: Cut 8 triangle pairs.
From dark green: Cut 16 triangle pairs.

Assembly

1. Make the drunkard's squares as shown.

Make 8 each.   Make 16.

2. Lay out and piece 8 four-patch path units with medium lavender backgrounds. These are just like the ones made for the light lavender path units, except you're using the darker lavender fabric for the wings.

Make 8.

Medium Lavender Star Units

Cutting

From medium lavender: Cut 24 small squares and 24 wing pairs.
From dark green: Cut 24 wing pairs.
From white: Cut 24 triangle pairs.
From dark print: Cut 48 triangle pairs.
From medium gold: Cut 20 wing pairs.
From light gold: Cut 4 wing pairs.

Assembly

1. Make the drunkard's squares as shown.

Make 24 each.   Make 20.   Make 4.

2. Layout the drunkard's squares and plain squares to make 12 four-patch units with medium gold wings and 12 with light gold wings.

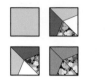

Make 12.

Make 12.

Light Green Star Units

Cutting

From light green: Cut 12 wing pairs and 12 small squares.
From dark green: Cut 12 wing pairs.
From white: Cut 12 triangle pairs.
From dark print: Cut 24 triangle pairs.
From medium gold: Cut 12 wing pairs.
From light lavender: Cut 4 large squares.

Assembly

1. Make the drunkard's squares as shown, paying careful attention to color placement.

Make 12 each.

2. Using 1 of each drunkard's square color combination and a light green plain square, lay out and piece a four-patch unit as shown. Repeat to make a total of 12 units.

Make 12.

Assembling the Quilt

1. Using the various four-patch units, lay them out in rows to assemble section A. Sew the rows together; then repeat to make another section A.

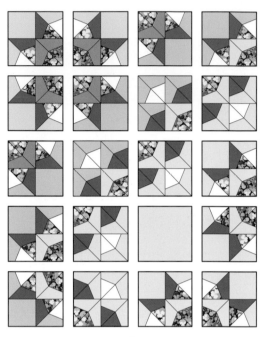

Section A
Make 2.

2. Using remaining four-patch units, lay out and assemble 2 of section B.

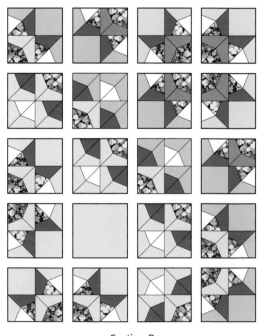

Section B
Make 2.

3. Lay out the quarters as shown so each corner of the quilt has a light green star. Sew the top left quarter to the bottom left quarter. Then sew the top right quarter to the bottom right quarter. Sewing the tops to the bottoms first will enable you to attach the long side borders without a seam in the middle.

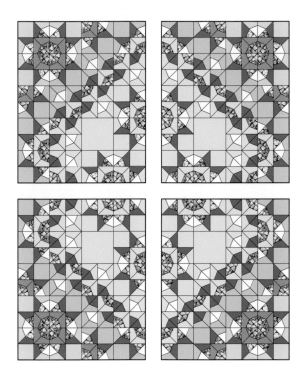

Border

Cutting

From dark lavender: Cut 2 outer border rectangles and 4 wing pairs.

From medium lavender: Cut 2 inner border rectangles, 8 small squares, and 4 wing pairs.

From medium green: Cut 4 miter strip pairs and 16 wing pairs.

From white: Cut 8 triangle pairs and 8 wing pairs.

From dark print: Cut 16 triangle pairs.

From medium gold: Cut 8 wing pairs.

From light green: Cut 4 miter strip pairs, 16 triangle pairs, and 4 small squares.

Assembly

1. Make the drunkard's squares as shown.

Make 4 each.   Make 8.

2. Sew the drunkard's squares and small medium-lavender squares together in four-patch units as shown.

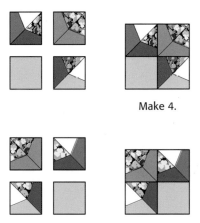

Make 4.

Make 4.

3. Make the drunkard's squares as shown.

Make 8 each.

4. Using the medium green and light green miter strips, the pairs of drunkard's squares made in step 2, the green drunkard's squares from step 3, and the plain light green squares, lay out and sew top and bottom border rows. Make 2 of each row shown and set them aside.

Top and Bottom Border
Make 2 each.

5. The side borders are made the same way as the top and bottom rows, except they have the medium and dark lavender rectangles inserted in the center. Make 2 of each row shown for the side borders.

Side Border
Make 2.

6. Sew the top and bottom border rows to the top and bottom of both halves of the quilt top.

7. Sew the side borders to the outside edges of each half of the quilt top. Make sure you sew them to the outer edges and not what will be the center of your quilt!

8. Sew the 2 halves of the quilt together along the center seam to complete the quilt top.

Quilt Plan

Finishing

LAYER AND BASTE your quilt top; then quilt by hand or machine. For specific details on quilting and binding, see "Techniques for Finishing," starting on page 16. You may also want to add a hanging sleeve and label to your quilt.

Patterns

Patterns include
¼" seam allowance.

2" Wing

2" Triangle

3" Wing

3" Triangle

4" Wing

4" Triangle

About the Author

Mary Sue Suit is a self-taught quiltmaker whose love of geometric designs led her to develop her own techniques and tools for creating patchwork quilts. her previous books, also published by Martingale & Company, are *All the Blocks are Geese* and *A New Twist on Triangles*. In addition, Mary Sue's work has been featured in *Quilter's Newsletter Magazine* and on the television show *Simply Quilts*. Mary Sue lives with her family in western Nebraska.